I0616391

Isn't That Weird!

Life lessons that will make you say...

Isn't That Weird!

SHELDON B. GOLDNER

Life lessons that will make you say...

Isn't That Weird!

by Sheldon B. Goldner

First Edition
Copyright © 2025 by Sheldon B. Goldner

Published by
Munn Avenue Press
300 Main Street, Ste 21
Madison, NJ 07940
MunnAvenuePress.com

Paperback ISBN: 978-1-969679-19-3
Hardcover ISBN: 978-1-969679-20-9

Printed in the United States of America

This book is dedicated to my youngest daughter Jodie. During her childhood, she and I would wander the world we lived in and marvel at how things happened and why. We often didn't know how things affected us or why they happened, and rather than look for some esoteric reason in the metaphysical world, we simply marveled at life, saying, "Wow, isn't that weird!"

That's the reason for the title of this book. Life throws so many things at us every day and most of us just say, "Wow, that was a rough day." Instead, I hope this book will allow you to understand that as you go through your day, whatever be your challenges and tasks within those common mundane everyday things that we do, there are signs, there are signals, and there is a universe trying to communicate with us in some finite way that perhaps we're not used to. But if you take a moment, if you just look for the signs, it is absolutely amazing, uncanny, spiritual, mystifying, unique, and yes, downright weird how things happen in our lives and make our lives become what they are. Weird, wonderful, wacky and great experiences every day will be yours if you are open to just seeing the signs and listening to the universe. So, stop fighting it and just go with the flow, as they say.

Jodie, although we have had our issues, always know that I love you. I'm always available to you and your sister Marnie as well. And remember, Jodie, you always were my favorite. You too, Marnie. And, of course, you too Corie, for sure.

Love,
Dad

CONTENTS

OVERVIEW

The purpose of this book is to share with you some of the life lessons I have learned. My perceptions about life, love, and the universe are being shared with you so you can better traverse your life and understand what this world is all about.

So, you're probably asking yourself why you should buy this book. The obvious reason to me is that I can use the money. But the more serious answer is that I have been very successful in my life. Don't get me wrong, now. I paid my dues and made mistakes but have made more good decisions than bad.

If you can drop your ego and your pride and take some of my lessons as a guide for your journey, then we will both benefit. Hopefully, as you go through your life, you might come across some of the signs the universe is showing you; if so, then I have done my job.

I have lived a long time—78 years. And I have, of course, screwed up a lot like many of us do. I would love to tell you all about life in 10 easy lessons, but it doesn't work that way. My life has evolved, as all our lives do. Lessons never stop, so embrace them. Let your guard down. Be open to the universe and enjoy the ride. I know I'm having a blast. It's amazing. It really is. None of us are getting out of this life alive, so enjoy it while you can. Carpe Diem.

CHAPTER ONE

Open Your Mind and Get out of Your Way

OK, OK, I'm writing it finally. This is the book I've been telling everyone I would write "eventually", called, *Life Lessons Learned That Will Make You Say, Isn't That Weird!* So, now it must be "eventually," because here we go.

Before we get into it in depth, please understand that this book is a "stream of consciousness," which means, to all of you out there, that what I think, I write. I hope it doesn't make this book difficult to read, and if it does, just deal with it. By the way, my humor is kind of tough and cutting. What that means is that I sometimes gently and lovingly tear someone's ass apart with sarcasm. (I'm only joking but there is always some truth in humor.)

Isn't That Weird refers to how life happens; in fact, in today's modern verbiage, this is sometimes reflected in the term "shit happens," but this is too simplistic a statement. It's much more than that. When I started to think about writing this book, I thought *Wow, I've got to write things down so I don't forget them,* but I quickly realized that these things happen every single day. All you must do is watch for the signs and signals that the universe is sending to you. It's like dialing into a radio station—you turn it left, you turn it right, then keep tweaking it until the station comes in loud and clear; welcome to the radio station called "The Universe." Don't worry Sparky, I'll explain all this to you later; it'll make much more sense.

I think it's important early on to explain signs and signals to you—perhaps some simple examples will set the scene. OK, so I was married for 42 years, a long time for sure, and then got divorced. At that point in my life, I guess the best description of me was that I was emotionally bankrupt. I quickly latched onto the first kind girl I had met in years. She seemed normal, if you will, and then the horror started. She tried hiding her problems for the first five years, but then she could no longer hide her true self from me. She turned out to be a thief and a liar, and to have borderline personality disorder and a drug addiction. What a nightmare she was!

She even faked having cancer and I just couldn't tolerate the prison I was in. I literally went from the frying pan to the fire. I thought, *What do I do now?* Done with her, I realized you can't change people. Remember all you people out there who are reading this—you cannot change anyone. Either you like who they are, or you don't. Don't compromise, or else you will settle for less than you want or deserve, and you will ultimately get what you deserve for shorting yourself. Maybe it's because you lack self-esteem that you feel you don't deserve any better. Either way, it's your choice and you will ultimately live with your decisions. It's not going to get better by hanging in there like I did. Don't waste your time; they are who they are, so don't try changing anyone. It just doesn't work.

So, what did I do next? Well, the dating sites of course, and that lasted for only a short time as I became so sick of women just posting headshots because their ass would fill up the picture, or using a photo that was 25 years old. Some of these women were forward enough to ask me how much money I made a year, what kind of car I drove, and even how big my home was! Crazy, huh?

So, enough of that source of females! I'd rather be celibate and all alone rather than be with some of these women. Now, I'm sure there are some decent, "honest" (again a definition word) women out there, but I didn't have the time or patience to sort them out. So, my mantra became, "I don't want any women to date; don't fix me up; I don't want telephone numbers; I'll finally meet somebody when the time is right."

The next part of the story is the first sign I will tell you about. Please remember, this is all true and these signs actually happened to me.

After a month or so, I got a phone call from a past friend of mine named Ken. He asked me if I would like to meet him for dinner along with his girlfriend. It seemed his girlfriend was bringing her best friend along, who happened to be visiting from out of town (I think she was from Seattle.) She wanted to introduce Ken to her girlfriend, and not wanting to have an odd-man-out situation, he asked me if I would like to have dinner with her along with him and his girlfriend— a foursome if you will. My knee-jerk reaction was to say to Ken, "No way, I don't want to be fixed up." I was sick and tired of getting taken advantage of by those crazy women out there, and of course I would say such things because I'm vain, conceited, shallow, and self-centered—what else would a normal man think?

Ken's immediate response was, "Then stay home; it was going to be a free dinner for you."

A free dinner offer from Ken—wow!

"Fuck you," he added.

Not wanting to miss out on a free dinner, especially from tight-ass Ken, I accepted.

Lesson to learn:

Don't be so structured with your day-to-day activities. Be open to meeting new people, interruptions, and doing new things with new friends. You will never see around the corner if you don't expand your walking distance.

CHAPTER TWO

Signs and Signals

Ken and his girlfriend Bianca drove to the restaurant in one car. Please keep track of this because it's important that you know the number of cars. So, right now we have Ken and Bianca in one car, the out-of-town girlfriend from Seattle in another car, and me in a third car. I brought some white roses, which is what Ken and I usually did whenever we met a new woman.

Vince, the manager of the restaurant, and I waited at the bar for my "date" to show up. I felt it best to be early because I didn't know what this woman looked like and I didn't want her waiting for me. I knew Ken was going to be late as he always was. In time, she appeared. Being in Chicago in late October, she was bundled up in a winter coat with collar up, a hat, a scarf around her face, and mittens. She didn't know whom to ask for since her girlfriend and Ken were not there yet. Typical Ken shit, always late, a control freak.

So, this woman was waiting at the hostess stand and I could hear her say, "I don't really know whom I'm asking for, as I'm supposed to meet some people here." With that, I walked up to her and gave her the white roses. It was certainly nothing romantic at this point for sure.

I said to her, "You must be Bianca's friend. I'm sorry, but I don't even know your name and I apologize for that."

With that, she said her name was Jamie. She accepted the flowers and Vince the manager escorted us to the table.

She was very tall—five foot, 10 inches—with blonde hair. As I said, she looked lost. Because she was bundled up, I didn't get a good look at her. Now, pay attention to what follows.

Once at the table, things changed rapidly as she took off her hat, scarf, and bulky winter coat. As each layer was removed, she unveiled a beautiful face with an amazing figure. Now, don't get me wrong. As I told you, I'm shallow at times, but I am a man; need I say more? And yet, I have to say more. Ken and Bianca finally arrived. As I found out later, my date Jamie was there to check out Ken because Bianca's picker has not been too good with men (we say kiddingly); she had been divorced twice and had also had some sociopathic boyfriends along the way. She couldn't pick the right man to save her life. Now, I'm a very out-there, type-A personality. I'm not shy; I love to talk to people, and there before me was a new person. Across from me, just waiting for me to pontificate on my worldly opinions of things, was this woman. But for some reason, I just kept staring at Jamie while making small talk. It was so unlike me; what was going on? And then it happened. (Remember, there are subtle signs that happen to all of us every day, every moment if we're just open to them.) This sign that I'm going to tell you about was not subtle. It was over the top and literally "in your face."

What started as a subtle sign quickly became almost supernatural. While I was making small talk, Jamie was speaking and replying, and she constantly kept asking Ken questions. All the time, it felt as if I were watching a scene at a restaurant table, with people speaking, yet I was separated from them, hovering over the table, looking down at all of them. This was weird—really weird, an extreme version of really weird. An overwhelming feeling came over me as I looked over at Jamie.

Her face was beautiful, but it was all blurry around her, like an aura.

I know this sounds corny, but I was smitten by this woman. Yes, call it as you may, I was falling for this woman, and I had only just met her. We only spoke a few words, but I was hooked. Call it love at first sight or whatever; I was not only falling in love, but I also knew that I would marry her. And believe me, after many, many years of an unhappy marriage, that was the last thing I wanted . . . or so I thought.

Jamie asked Ken all kinds of questions while I stayed somewhat quiet throughout dinner. When it was time to leave, which was extremely late as I think we closed down the restaurant with our talking, I had a bit of a problem. I felt dazed and confused, and l actually stumbled to my car. By the way, I don't drink so it was something else that I was dazed about and not alcohol. Remember, there were three cars at the restaurant. They were parked all over the lot, and we were the last three cars in the lot. Since we were the last ones to leave, I just walked over to my car and before I got in, I looked over at Ken's car and they were all saying goodbye to each other.

What was I thinking? How rude of me! I quickly went over to the three of them and said good night as well. I mumbled something, then got in my car and drove home.

The whole way home, I thought, *What's with this moment, this evening?* It was all so surreal, what happened to me. Who was this girl? I didn't even get her phone number. I went to sleep that night but couldn't get her out of my mind. I had to see her again. I called Ken's girlfriend Bianca and asked for Jamie's cell phone number. She told me she would have to ask Jamie, so I had to wait. Being patient is not easy for me but wait I had to.

I could go on and on about Jamie and my pursuit to win her over. In fact, while on our third date, I believe she said to me that before this relationship went any further, she had to tell me something; she, in her not-so-immediate future but in her future nevertheless, wanted to marry again, even after two failed marriages in the past. If I had no interest in an eventual marriage, she said, "Please do not pursue me." You can call it spirituality or whatever. But the words just came out, "I have no problem with marrying you if you are indeed the right person."

I couldn't believe I blurted that out! I followed up with, "I have no problem with marriage; it's the divorce part that I don't enjoy." Please understand that I was so smitten by this woman that I already knew I would do just that—marry her! Wow, talk about a sign.

I'm rambling, but I will tell you that we got married on 3/23/23! That's why this information about her and my strange and mysterious thoughts on the evening we met were for sure an extreme and vivid sign from the universe. Most signs are much more subtle, as they happen every single day and only if you are receptive to the signs from the universe will you even be aware of them. Jamie and I often say that it's unfortunate there are so many people out there who are asleep. They go through their day, waking up in the morning, stumbling to their car; they can't even remember how they got to work. They do their eight hours with the appropriate lunch break, and then, like zombies, drive back home, watch some TV after dinner, and go to bed . . . rinse and repeat, rinse and repeat.

This ain't living, Sparky. It's called sleeping and being oblivious to any signs. How could you see a sign when you don't even remember how you drove home, but nevertheless you did, and in your "walk-around coma," got ready for dinner.

> ### *Lesson to learn:*
> Don't be afraid of where your mind takes you. Let it go and see where it takes you because the universe knows better than us. Read on and you will understand more.

CHAPTER THREE

More of the Same

So, let's look at some signs; there are more every day. Sometimes, the universe sees what we are doing and wants us to stop for whatever reason. The universe doesn't send text messages; instead, it sends you signs in a very subtle way. Here's a good example: I was given a stock tip from a cousin of Jamie's who had the inside track on a company; it was a penny stock that was being offered at $0.25 a share. I watched it for quite a few months and left it alone. I did some research on it and concluded that this company had so many problems it would never stay in business. I concluded that it was a loser, and I'm too smart to be suckered in, so I ignored it and months went by. I remembered that Jamie had bought some stock, but she never said anything about it.

Casually, I asked her how that stock was doing. She said she hadn't wanted to mention it to me before because she knew how I felt about the company and such. I really wanted to know about it.

Curious, I asked smugly, "How much is it worth now?" expecting it to be below the purchase price of $0.25 per share.

"Oh, it's done pretty well," was her response. "It's at $1.40 per share."

I thought I'd choke! I looked at the stock and it had been on a tear. For those of you who don't know what FOMO means, it stands for "fear of missing out." I was too smart to lose this opportunity, so I called my broker and bought a substantial amount of the stock at $1.40, and of course, we all know what happened.

It was as if the stock was waiting for me, and only me, to invest. Once I was in, the stock plummeted to $0.20 a share and eventually down to .15 a share. The universe had told me not to do it, but I ignored the sign. Oh yes, not the sign but rather the SIGNS—all of them. When I decided to buy the stock, I had some difficulties. First, before I could execute the trade, my computer crashed. Then I tried my cell phone and the brokerage house's platform crashed. Next, I couldn't execute my trade due to something technical and then the site finally returned. But I knew better . . . screw the universe and its signs! Although I should have looked for the signs, I didn't. The universe tried to tell me, but I didn't listen.

Sometimes, you must stop and reflect on what's going on around you. The universe knows and tries to tell us, but it's up to us to listen and watch for the signs.

Here is another sign that I *did* listen to. I had been in business for over 45 years before I retired. So, I learned a few things along the way—not in the early years when I didn't know about signs, but in the last several years, or at least since I met Jamie.

During that time, I had many business deals come to me. Sometimes you try to do a deal, but it doesn't work. For whatever reason, there's a problem with the deal. You can try to go over the deal, you can try to go under it or around it, but alas, no go. And believe me, I have had a lot of those in my career. They take forever but the results are always the same: NADA. And then other times, when the stars seem to align and the universe smiles at us, it works. The deal is completed, and ever so effortlessly. As I like to say, "When it goes, it flows."

I had no idea about signs back then. I learned the hard way. So, here is another example of applying my past experiences to today. I recently tried to open an Instagram account. What a nightmare! I tried this and I tried that, but whatever I tried, it wouldn't work. Perhaps it was because I'm technologically challenged, but for whatever reason, it was a no-go. I was going to ask Jamie for her help but then stopped myself. The universe was once again speaking to me, and I was refusing to listen. But not this time—no, no, no, not this time. No way.

You see, many of us have family and friends who don't really want happiness for us. They want you happy, but they just don't want you *too* happy. So, I thought, *Why bother?*, especially since the universe was sending signs by making it difficult to sign up with Instagram. Finally, I was learning my lessons by listening to the signs. I didn't and don't know what could have happened if I had joined up on Instagram, but I wasn't tempting fate. I was starting to learn about signs, and the universe was trying to tell me something. I finally became open to the vibrations of the universe.

Lesson to learn:

Trust yourself and trust your gut. Don't believe in the so-called experts who say they know better than us. They put their pants on the same way we do and unless they're a professional person who has had special schooling, their opinion is probably no better than ours. So, if you have a decision to make, look into yourself and ask yourself what your gut says. More than likely, your gut will be right. Believe in you. You're more than you realize.

CHAPTER FOUR

You Too, Brutus?

I sometimes think that even some of my people would be happier to have me, at 78 years old, just sit in my apartment until I start drooling and then put me into a care facility so they don't have to bother with me. Some people just hate to see others happy and would rather have everyone else stay with them in their 55-gallon drum of bad attitude. Whatever. It's not going to happen . . . especially not with my own money!

You see, I have family members who work for me. They do a great job, and I am a great believer in nepotism. I mean, after all, I've got to pay somebody and pay the tax man if I make money, so I'd rather give it to people I care about. But as they say, no good deed goes unpunished. If I asked anybody but those who work for me, "Are friends and family who work for me overpaid for what they do?", the answer would be "Of course, they are *way* overpaid for what they do." Don't be upset when you hear such words, because what would you expect someone to say? Most people think the other guy is overpaid and they are underpaid. This is human nature—one man's perspective.

If you ask my family members who work for me whether they are overpaid, they'll say, "Of course not; we're underpaid, and we should make more!" If they're reading this, they can be pissed if they want, but this is just my viewpoint; it's not right or wrong. They might think, *Without us, there would be no business.* Maybe they're right, but it's just the way it works; no need to get all riled up. It's just the way life is—everyone thinks they're more valuable than they really are. It's human nature. You can't blame anybody, and I'm not mad. It's kind of like driving—we all think we're better than the average driver . . . again, that's human nature.

But that's OK because I love these people and I care about them. I don't want them to have to struggle as much as I had to. A little bit of struggle is OK, though; they live in a beautiful home and drive two nice cars—a Porsche and a big Audi SUV. Gas is a company benefit as is their health insurance, and I think one car is paid for by the company, or maybe two, but I don't recall. You see, my attitude about money is kind of cavalier. I told them from early on, "Please take what you need but leave some for me." If they bleed the company, then I'm the last one to get cut, so they should watch the cash flow and enjoy it. Again, they do a great job and allow me to be retired. I appreciate and love them both.

Enjoy it they do, and don't get me wrong; they have a great work ethic—much more than their peers but certainly nowhere near my generation. We're just wired differently and that I accept. When I went through my divorce, my son-in-law was the only one, and I mean the *only* one who called me up that evening and said the words that have always embodied his loyalty and branded it forever: "Are you OK?" Those few words meant the world to me, especially at that moment in time. Remember, people, life is about moments, so embrace them all, both good and bad.

Many people just weren't happy with my decision about a divorce, but that's *my* problem, and *my* worries in my life so I'm not going to bother you with that. Believe me, some things are difficult for us to swallow but swallow we must. Some of my daughters stopped speaking to me because of the divorce. One daughter finally came around after quite a bit of time, but understand, I have no hate for any of my kids. I don't want you to think I'm that *big* of an *******, although I am an *******—no doubt about that.

When my son-in-law came to me, he was a struggling attorney making dollars per hour. He has come a long way, and although I could have hired a CEO to replace me, I now look at him and ask myself, "How could I ever replace him?"

I could be wrong, but it seems to me that most people do not like change. However, the one constant thing in life is change. It happens. We can't control it, and we must be Darwinian. What that means is that with change as inevitable as it is, we must, as Darwin said, adapt or die. In fact, we absolutely must adapt to change as we can't control it, so let's get flexible Frankie, change is coming, whether it be technology or your relationships. Things continue to evolve whether we like it or not, both good things and bad things. Believe it!

So, when certain friends and family members found out about Jamie, they freaked out. Not about Jamie per se; it could have been Susie or Kate or anyone. It was just that if I was finding another woman in my life after a 42-year marriage and a way-too-long, even worse relationship after that, then what could be next? *Another divorce if he marries another winner .. . oy vey!* (for the Yids; no, I didn't mean kids. I meant to say Yids. Forget about it; my people know what I mean!)

What does this mean to my friends and family members? *Is there another divorce on the horizon? Does this mean more expenses for the company? He must be crazy!* Now again, everything in life is about perspective, so how I view things, the decisions I have made, and what they mean to me are mine. Strictly mine—my perceptions, my reality, my emotions, my responses. So, please understand this. My life, my FUCK-UP. Then so fuckin' be it. It is what it is, and that, Sparky, is another universal rule. IT IS WHAT IT IS, so suck it up, buttercup, and do the Nike thing: to undo the wrong, JUST DO IT!. Sorry, but I do ramble from time to time. Ok moving forward....

So, back to Jamie and wanting people to be happy for me. As I said, certain friends and family members freaked out. So, I had the feeling that everyone was mad at me, all because for the first time in my life, I was putting *me* first and giving myself permission to be happy. It was so unlike me. It is what it is, remember? Life is mystical. But there is one thing that all these naysayers had in common: they were all really mad at me. To that, I had to say I didn't give a damn about what they thought. If I screw up, it's my screw-up. My money, my heartache, my life. Rambling again, aren't I?

I don't know what it is about all of us, myself included, but we all seem to go to the negative, like a knee-jerk reaction. So, I think I'm going to give my friends and family the benefit of the doubt because at this moment in time, I'm no different than them. I do the same thing they do. In fact, if I were in their place, I also would have told me I was nuts. Everyone goes to the negative! But as I said before, it's my money, my heartache, and my life if I make a mistake.

So, back to our above reality. Everyone, for some reason, went immediately to thoughts of another divorce: more lawyers, more legal bills, and above all else, changes that could affect them. I hate to wake everybody up, but this is *my* story I'm writing. People don't think of me first; they think about how this is going to affect them. Am I just collateral damage? It's all just human nature; we default to the worst-case scenario, and that's just the way it is. Just don't overthink it. No malice here.

At least to me, it seemed they were all really pissed. But they needed to tell somebody else about it, because I really didn't give a damn about what they thought. I sometimes don't understand human nature. Why did everyone go immediately to the negative instead of saying, "Oh, he finally found love. Isn't that wonderful?" Like I said, we all default to the worst-case scenario, and I'm just as guilty. I don't know what goes through people's minds, but it could be that they think, *If he marries, then she or someone else will get our inheritance, or at least a good chunk of it.* I love that "our inheritance" crap, as if any of us are promised or entitled to receive anything.

I mean, come on; all of us would like to be the one who says, "Wow, this is a great life story. It could have been a movie—he finally found love. Isn't it wonderful! The guy (me) has been through a lot; he never quit trying until he found what he wanted. Good for him." Nope! Instead, they only think the worst. That's just the way it is. We've got to laugh at that.

Because let's face it, friends, we all subconsciously wish we were that kind of guy: fighting for what he believes in, pursuing his dreams, never happy, no matter how old this guy is, and what the hell—everyone loves a good hero story, especially when the guy ends up like this guy did.

Yeah, it's me. He marries his beautiful girlfriend, retires to Hawaii, and lives way longer than his ex-wife and girlfriends expected or wanted him to (lol), and loves his life and his wife. You can't make this stuff up. WOW, there is a universe!

> *Lesson to learn (a long but important lesson for sure):*
> Stay the course. Keep focused on what you and your heart are telling you. be laser-focused, sharp-focused. Don't expect others to understand what your gut is telling YOU. Be secure with your own thoughts. You make the decisions—you, as lonely as it can be, and stay the course. This is going to be difficult at first, as we all like to go with the crowd. Unfortunately, that has never worked out well for me. Even if I was with the crowd, I was usually miserable because it wasn't my decision, it was theirs: the others and me, just one of the sheep.

Harvard University did a study about gut feelings in situations we all have been in. After all their analysis, the conclusion was that 86% of the time, our gut feelings are right. I can't tell you how many times I let others tell me what I should do when it came to making a decision. Maybe I thought they all knew better than I did, but in reality, now that I am old, I realize that my decisions were as good as anybody else's. In fact, they were better, because I knew myself better than anyone else. From the time the Pilgrims landed on Plymouth Rock, to the current state of affairs, we have all had to make decisions based on our gut feelings. My experiences taught me that the so-called experts who knew better than everybody were nothing more than tongues looking for a job and a paycheck.

Don't get me wrong. There are experts such as doctors, but they are not absolute in their decisions either. They always say, "Get a second opinion."

They say small children and animals can sense the good or evil in people. Have you ever met somebody, and you get a feeling in your gut that this is not a good person, that there is something wrong or just not quite right about them? The answer is usually shown to us at a later time, but what I'm telling you is to go with those feelings. Do not be so open and accepting because of social norms, or whatever the reason, especially if the person carries a title or wears a white coat. Titles and appearances are always a warning sign, so be careful how you approach them. He is not better than you are. He doesn't know how to do your job, and you certainly can't do his. That's OK. When people show who they really are the first time, believe it or it'll be a hell of a lot more painful later on. This is your life, and you will pay the price for making a bad decision. So, listen to your gut.

Let me tell you about my brother whom I affectionately called jerk-off. He was my accountant; remember, an accountant is supposed to be an expert. I told him I wanted to invest $10,000 into something called the Magellan fund. Why he decided to tell me differently, I'm not sure. His response to me was, "Oh no, my partner here in the accounting firm is investing in a fund by the name of the XYZ fund, and it's doing great."

Understand that I had done my own research. I had checked out the fund manager's performance and history. I had done my own due diligence. I had read everything I could about the Magellan fund. And yet, even though I had done all my due diligence, I still did not trust my gut and my knowledge about the Magellan fund. No, I thought. Somebody else must know better than I do.

So, what happened? I invested the $10,000 into the XYZ fund, lost my ass, and the Magellan fund always bragged about how a $10,000 investment around that time turned into well over $1 million in less than 10 years. Do you see the trend here? Follow your gut and rely on you, because then it's only you that can be blamed if things don't go the way you thought. You won't be surprised. You might be quite pleased with your performance and your decisions, but if you screw up, it's your screw-up. And besides, the more times you are right, the more confidence you will gain in your own decisions; remember the Harvard 86% theory research.

CHAPTER FIVE

Subtle Signs Are Still Signs

I just put my journal away as I am waiting for a flight to Brazil, but I had another very interpretive sign from the universe. Sometimes the signs are from a song, and when you listen to the words of that song, you believe that the artist wrote the song directly to you and you alone. Of course, other times, it's just a song. You've got to listen and be aware and see if something out in this universe is trying to tell you something; if it is, you must be open. Not only to what you are hearing but also to what you're not hearing.

There is a song by Diana Ross called "My Turn." Her words talk about her journey and going on her life path by herself. And on this journey, she knows there will be problems: the rain will fall upon her, and there are trials and tribulations, but she must go by herself because it's just that—it's her life's journey. I heard this song when I had left my father-in-law, working in the seafood business. I knew what I had to do, and that song reaffirmed it for me. I didn't realize at that time that it was a sign from the universe telling me, "It's OK. Go you must; go on your own path." This is just an example of musical signs you might hear . . . but I ramble again.

I read something recently that I wanted to share with you. It's not about music, but it's just some thoughts that I found quite unique. So, here we go on a little bit of a different path.

I read something that said: As you go through your life journey, many people, friends and/or family, come along with you. Sometimes things change and sometimes, just sometimes, you decide that it's time to leave these people on the side of the road as you continue. It's just that their thoughts don't align with yours anymore because you're on *your* journey. So, leave them on the side of the road. It matters not who they are: mother, father, sister, brother, or best friend. It doesn't matter.

These people will often look at you questioningly and say, "What's wrong with you? You've changed." But the truth of the matter is, you haven't changed. You have just grown, and they will not understand. This is also good for them, but at this time of the relationship, they will not see it as such, as they will usually be hurt or pissed off at you. So, leave them on the side of the road; it's just time to do so. It's good for you and although it may not appear to be as good for them in the long run, it is. When they were good for you, it was good, but move on you must.

So, let me share this with you. Remember that I had only one daughter out of three that was speaking to me after I decided to get divorced. Of course, she works for me, and that might be the only reason. For 13 years or so, from the moment I stated I wanted to divorce, I had been asking this daughter for lunch or dinner or just to meet with me one-on-one so I could explain my position. Nope, she was always too busy and had one excuse after another. Finally, after I saw a shrink and learned that you can't change people or control them, I had had enough. Nothing was working. I had to do something radical.

Boundaries needed to be put into place. I called my daughter and set those boundaries. Finally, I told her I didn't like the way I had been treated by her and that I didn't want to see her again or talk with her. I told her that her family was dead to me, and I wanted nothing to do with them. I needed to shock her and shock her I did. I think she had no idea how I was feeling, and how things looked from my perspective. Whatever the reason, it shocked her back into reality All of a sudden, she wanted to have lunch, dinner, or anything so we could talk. Maybe she was scared she would be fired or left out of the will, whatever. We met, we spoke, and we started to rebuild our relationship, and for the first time in 13 years, she allowed me to be a grandfather as well. She and I took the kids out for the day, and I was able to spend time with them and spoil them. It was a heartwarming day for me after 13 years of being an outcast to my family.

Listen, I'm not a prick. I have a big heart, and I've always shared what I have with others, even many who never deserved my kindness and generosity. Now, I text her and she texts back right away. Or just out of the blue, she will text me to ask how I'm doing. Nice, huh? The little things make a big difference.

But not so fast. Remember, I told you some of the signs from the universe are silent and we must be astute enough to recognize the silence as a sign in itself? Remember I told you how Jamie came into my life? Well, let me explain to you about that.

I told the only daughter who is talking to me about Jamie, and I mentioned the same thing to my son-in-law. I even promoted Jamie to my daughter as someone special with a brain, and that it was serious. Before you read the following, I do feel that my daughter and son-in-law were trying to protect me; that they thought my judgment was flawed, and they weren't confident about any decision I might make.

We all went to dinner; my daughter was cordial and that's it. My son-in-law was avoidant and cold, and both of them were tolerating Jamie and couldn't wait for dinner to be over. Even Ray Charles could see the strained evening! It was not exactly a warm dinner, and perhaps that's what's best to say because I'm sure they will read this. It was obvious and apparent to me that neither of them were thrilled with Jamie, but it wasn't her personally; it would've been anybody I had said those words about. Let's say they were being protectively cautious. Again, why be happy for me if it would probably end in divorce anyway and cost them money from their entitled inheritance? And now for the real thing that really, *really* pissed me off and HURT me. (Believe me, you don't ever want to piss me off, ever!)

After that dinner, Jamie, who would love family to be like a Norman Rockwell painting, said to me, "Stop, please stop promoting me as you don't have to sell me to anyone. Attraction, not promotion." I listened and agreed. No more mention of her going forward as there is another character in this diatribe—my son-in-law's mother. She's from New York and she has a heart of gold. She's a great mother to my son-in-law, loves my daughter, and is a great grandmother to my grandchildren. But there is a side to her that one should be aware of; she has said so herself.

She always says she was the "bad child "in school, and you didn't want to mess with her. After all, she *is* from New York.

Fast forward: Jamie and I were out for an evening, and I could tell she was upset about something. "What's up?" I asked as I like to know the problem before it escalates. She told me reluctantly that she got a call from a very good friend of hers and was told that this friend's husband was a good friend of a guy Jamie dated before me. The story goes that this past boyfriend was contacted by a guy named Adam. Adam wanted to know some information from this past boyfriend about Jamie, and had either met with, or talked on the phone with my son-in-law's mother, my son-in-law, and/or my daughter. He said the family was concerned about the influence of Jamie on me and asked what kind of person she was. Was she looking for money? Was she of good character? What influence could she have on me? Was she a quality person? On, and on, and on the questions persisted.

Adam repeated to the ex-boyfriend that the family was very concerned.

This took a lot of nerve, didn't it? Not only did they, or she, or whomever was willing to take the opinion of a former boyfriend—who most likely wouldn't give a glowing report due to his relationship with Jamie ending—but they were not willing to form their own impression and opinion of Jamie by getting to know her themselves. How foolish of them.

Not that it matters, but I'm a stand-up guy to know that the ex-boyfriend deserves kudos. He said he realized the family was "concerned about her," but he was sharp enough to say that Jamie was a quality person, and he didn't want to get involved. "He said, she said," and all the other nonsense of gossip. I think Adam concluded that he didn't get enough information, so he had to say *something*. In his opinion, he said, there was probably something not right about her, and she wasn't a quality person. What he based that on, I'm not really sure. Remember, we always go to the negative when we don't know facts, so it must've sounded better to say that Jamie wasn't 100% rather than give her a glowing report. They decided to rely on somebody else for an opinion they themselves should have made. As you can tell, I was and still am hot about those behind-the-scenes discussions. The nerve of them, not wanting to make a decision based on their own experiences with her.

But in their defense, and I always try to look at the other person's perspective, they were just trying to help. Whether it be the mother-in-law, or the son-in-law, or my daughter, or whomever, they were all distraught and only inquired for the "good" of the family. That is why I say to my family, I understand and to Adam, Fuck you.

I always like to give people the benefit of the doubt, so maybe they were just concerned for me. But what the fuck? How insulting and devious of all of them! Well, I'm not going to hold back my mouth, which has gotten me into all sorts of trouble in my life, as well as making me a shit-load of money.

I called my daughter and confronted her about what Jamie had said. She absolutely denied knowing anything about it: "I don't know what she's talking about; that couldn't be true," and on and on. Obviously, I've known this child all her life, and she was one of the only ones that never lied to me, or so I thought. So, she might have been truthful. I could have done it without a watch, but after I hung up with her, I said to myself, "10-9-8-7, etc. By the time I got to zero, the phone was ringing. It was my son-in-law's mother and she wanted to know how I was. How are you? How is Jamie? We must get together sooner than later. Then, it was my daughter's turn: "Hey Dad, let's all get together. You must bring Jamie by; we have to get to know her," and blah, blah. They would've been better served by telling me they fucked up and were sorry. It was all denials, but the damage was done. Jamie felt hurt. I was pissed, and now, for sure, I will do what I feel is best for Jamie and me.

Family can be wonderful, and they can be a pain in the ass. Especially if what you do affects them in some way. So, remember that no one, *no one* likes change, and a new actor or actress like Jamie in the fold is change in itself. My daughter stopped texting and calling me; all of a sudden, she was too busy for me. This has gone on for the last 13 years, and remember, silence can be a sign in itself. When the pattern of your life changes, it is a sign. Don't run from it; don't go to the dark side. It's funny about human nature—for some reason, and it happens to all of us, we jump to the worst-case scenario:

My daughter stopped calling so she must be mad at me, or, *The Uber driver was late; what a jerk*, or, *A waitress served me a salad without a fork, how stupid of her*, when the truth was that my daughter had an emergency with the kids and couldn't call, the Uber driver had an accident and was sending another car, and the waitress went to get a clean fork as the one she was going to place before me was dirty. So, why do we make these assumptions like knee-jerk reactions? Again, it's human nature. We all do it, even me. I know I'm being redundant and am repeating this message over and over, but it's important to remember: No one likes change; a new actor or actress in the fold is change; silence can be a sign in itself; when the pattern of your life changes, it's a sign.

I am 78 years old, and I've had my share of life experiences. I finally figured out my perspective on life, and I do mean MY perspective.

So you understand that signs are very, very important, but you must be open and willing to receive them. If you think this is all bullshit, then stop now. Hopefully you paid for this book and didn't steal it, so if it is true that you think it's bullshit, then screw you, because you don't deserve my insight and probably would not be receptive to the signs that touch us all anyway.

I don't want to belabor the signs and their importance. Remember that the signs are coming from the universe, or from God, or from some deity of sorts. I'm not sure of the actual source, but I do know they are real, as they happen every single day. I think they guide us down our path of life. They seem to show us the reasons for things, and give us guidance, and sometimes reaffirm that the decisions we are making are correct, or that whatever it is we're contemplating is right or wrong for us—just us; it's very personal. Just for the record: In hindsight, when I look back at that time, I really do believe my son-in-law and daughter and family were looking out for me. Perhaps they felt my judgment had been flawed, or that maybe I was just too old to make a rational decision. Of course, I had made some mistakes in the past. I think they had my best interest at heart, and I love them for that. So to all of them reading this, don't be mad at me. I'm 78, so cut me some slack. And by the way, Jamie and all of them have a relationship that has blossomed nicely and respectfully as it continues to grow.

Lesson to learn:

Be true to yourself, as you are not a stupid person. You didn't live this long by being dumb. While others might be held in higher regard, your opinion matters as well.

Make your own decisions. Do not defer to the words of others. You know yourself better than anyone. No one can make conclusions or decisions for you because they are not you, and their perspective is not yours. Remember other people's opinions are just that—opinions. When you have a life decision to make, do so by yourself because others are not walking in your shoes and others do not know all the facts. You must rely on you. Notice the common thread throughout all these lessons you are learning?

CHAPTER SIX

Psychics and a Trip to Brazil

I've always enjoyed psychics, fortune-tellers, and card-readers. Now I know you probably think they are bullshit but let me tell you something. There are people out in the world who are extremely sensitive to the universe. Let's say people like this can pick up on the signs before we are even touched by them. One psychic said to me that I was blessed and so lucky to have Michael on my side. "Who the hell is Michael?" asked the naïve Jewish boy (me). I said this to the card reader/psychic without the vulgarity.

She told me it didn't matter that I was Jewish, and by the way, I never told her I was. She informed me that Michael was God's most favorite and powerful angel and that he had taken me under his wing. Kind of weird, isn't it? Let me tell you that I have gotten myself into some deep shit, whether it was personal, business, or whatever, and as dark as the day became, I always, always knew in my heart that I would figure it out, and I always have. When someone once said to me, "You're such an asshole, they should throw you to the wolves," my immediate response was, "That's OK, because if they do, I know I'll come out leading the pack." This has been my life; why, I don't know. What I *do* know is that Michael has always watched over me, and I am ever so grateful for him in the universe (but more about being grateful in another chapter.)

So, before we leave the discussion about signs, I'm going to share with you what signs appeared to me in just one 24-hour day. Believe me, I can't make this shit up. This actually happened to me.

I recently traveled to Brazil with Jamie to visit some of her friends. This woman of mine (Jamie) has touched many people, either as a professional ballerina in her youth, as a professional yoga instructor for 25 years, and as a student of yoga, with world-famous yoga instructors in India. The names of those she studied under are David Life, Sharon Gannon, Shawn Corn, and Rod Stryker, just to name a few. But the greatest honor for her was to study under Janis Cadwell for 10 years. I don't know about you, but to me, those names don't mean anything. However, when I witness her speaking these names to people in the yoga community, they are more than blown away; they are really impressed. I guess it's different strokes for different folks.

Anyway, there we were in Brazil, which for me was 7700 miles away from my bagel and lox upbringing, so I was learning more about this world in a universe with the woman of my dreams. She is a force to be reckoned with, and after I met her, I soon realized that I had better get on the train of exploration and learn about other cultures. If I resisted, I stood a good chance of being left at the station in some foreign land. Luckily for me, I love living out of a suitcase, at least metaphorically. I'm not complaining, as we live half the year on the big island of Hawaii, and the other half, we travel, so it's not a bad life. We are definitely world travelers.

During my first year of retirement, we went to India to visit Rishikesh, the birthplace of yoga. We saw Jaipur and Agra, where the Taj Mahal is, one of the wonders of the world. We visited Sri Lanka on the way to the Maldives, where we scuba dove for two weeks straight. We probably did 50 dives each while in the Maldives, and we got Nitrox-certified, along with receiving our advanced open- water certifications. We are currently, as of this writing, in Brazil in the most beautiful city called Curitiba.

I'm sorry to jump around with this book's content, but I did warn you that this would be stream of consciousness, so divert for a moment. As I told you, we are in Brazil for about two weeks and loving it. By the way, we are coming back at the end of 2023 to visit Brazil again: Rio, the Amazon, São Paulo, and some islands for more scuba diving along the way. Obviously, we love to travel. Before the trip to Brazil, I had mentioned to some friends that I was going there. Wow, you would have thought I told them I was going to Mars to visit Elon Musk.

"Are you crazy?" said one of my friends. "I know of a guy who went to Brazil and got kidnapped and then murdered. They never found the body!" Another friend sent me some stuff from the State Department, telling Americans to be aware of potential dangers in Brazil. I said nothing back to them at that moment, but I reflected on their words.

In Chicago, where I lived for 75 years, it's well documented that there are from 20 to 25 murders every fucking weekend, and brazen theft in the most exclusive shopping areas on Michigan Avenue where Gucci, Prada, Louis Vuitton, and other high-end retailers are located. These vandals even get on social media and tell everybody to join in, and then hundreds of looters get together and descend on retailers who can no longer defend themselves. They invite other animals out there to join in on this or that date and time; they get together as a mob and decimate our high-end retail stores, where the "good stuff" is literally free for the taking. Thank you, Mayor Laurie Lightfoot!

In fact, the friend who sent me the crap from the State Department is an investor in a high-end restaurant in downtown Chicago. We were all going to go there one weekend for dinner, but my friend received a call from the restaurant before we set out. The caller said, "You'd better not come down, as someone was just gunned down in front of our restaurant and the police are all over the place."

I wonder why retailers are closing up and moving out of Chicago? Duh!

Maybe you can help me out here. Is it Brazil that is so dangerous, or is it Chicago, where we have lived for our whole lives? We always default to the worst-case scenario rather than looking at our own perspectives and questioning ourselves. This aspect of human nature seems to be a common thread throughout this book. Dangerous my ass, look in your own backyard and not at Brazil. The world can be a dangerous place if you're stupid and you get drunk and you go to areas where you shouldn't be at two in the morning. Yes, it can be very dangerous, but for the most part, common sense prevails, and I do realize that common sense is not common . . . but nevertheless. It's also a beautiful world, and there are a lot of nice people in it. Thank God more nice people than bad people exist, so I'll take my chances going forth.

And one more deviation from the flow of this book: I sent a friend of mine named Paul some pictures of India. I describe the country as "beauty in chaos."

India has two billion people and not one McDonald's! Cows are holy in the Indian culture, and it is a fascinating culture. I sent Paul pictures of the people, the sites, and the culture. His response was, "Wow, so the struggles are real?" He was feeling sorry for the Indian people, actually feeling *really* sorry for them.

I responded that he was feeling pity for them and for their "struggle," but he could not be more wrong. I said the people were beautiful. All the women wear colorful garb. The men are so handsome with their black hair, beautiful, precise beards, and mustaches. The children, both boys and girls, all have great big dark eyes, and are so beautiful. The people are clean and stand tall, although they are much smaller in size than those in the US, and their clothes are clean and pressed. They have such pride, and it's apparent that they are all so happy, even with 99% of them having arranged marriages. You can tell they are happy, and happy about family, as family is everything in India. The people are gracious and beautiful. The culture is also beautiful, and the sights are something to behold. The food is too spicy for me; I lost 15 pounds during my two weeks there. How do they eat? They love spicy food. I loved the peanut butter and jelly sandwiches I made every day in the hotel where I stayed. Thank God for them!

I texted Paul back and said, "I don't understand. What is their struggle? Let me tell you, Paul, that the way I think you're viewing my pictures is that the people you are looking at have so few material goods, they must be very unhappy, and if someone has an abundance of things, they must be happy. That's fucked up and so shallow." I told Paul that all throughout my time in India, I didn't see one big-screen TV or any fancy cars or other signs of luxury. But guess what? The people are happy without those things. Paul hasn't responded to me since I told him how shallow his thinking is. I hope he is still my friend (lol).

Speaking of nice-looking things, let's talk about nice-looking people. I told you that the people of India are comparatively smaller in size to the people of the United States, dark skinned with dark hair. Jamie is 5'10" tall, light-skinned and blonde; she is stunning to say the least, and with a body that won't quit. Me, I'm a looker too, or so I think. Wherever we went in India, I watched the men's eyes. They would sneak a glance at her, but did so very respectfully. The Indian men are respectful and conservative, especially in their manners and especially when they were with their wives!

They must have thought Jamie was an oddity. Wherever we went, whether it be big cities or rural towns, orphanages, or schools Jamie helps support, everybody wanted a selfie with us. Well, not all of us. They would say to me, "Sir, not you, just her with us," and I had to get out of the picture, lol! WTF!

OK, back to where we were. These are my perspectives of signs within a 24-hour day. So, we are in Brazil in a city south of São Paulo called Curitiba, which is in the south of Brazil. It is 7700 miles from our home in Hawaii, so it's not like I know anyone from there. So, one day, while we were rocking this Brazilian city, we went into a pharmacy to try to buy some supplies and medicines for Jamie, as she and I had some minor plastic surgery. Plastic surgery is a big business in Brazil because of the exchange rate. I had priced out what they would charge for similar surgeries in the US, and it was $70,000. In Curitiba . . . wait for it . . . that same surgery cost $13,000! I found that unbelievable.

So, in the pharmacy we were trying to get some creams and medicines that the doctor had recommended, and we had a problem with translation. A woman standing right next to me offered her help as she spoke English perfectly. She was right next to me in the aisle when I was talking to Jamie. Remember, I said *right next to me,* not down the aisle, not in the next aisle, but right beside me. She helped us with the purchase and we spoke. I asked her, "How is it that your English is so perfect and yet you live here?"

"Oh, she said, "I worked for an American company, and I was stationed in the US for over a year."

Just being courteous, I asked her, "What company did you work for?"

"Oh," she said, "I'm sure you've never heard of it."

I persisted. "No, I'm curious. What's the name of the company?"

"Lubrizol," she said.

A smile came over my face, and now it was her time to contemplate my smug-looking face. "Oh, I know your company," I said.

"What do you know about the Lubrizol company?" she asked.

"Oh, I know quite a bit about Lubrizol. Let me tell you . . . Cleveland, Ohio, right? Your company bought a company in Rockton, Illinois named

Chemtool. Yes indeed, and there was a huge fire that took down the plant, and it was devastating. It destroyed the entire plant."

Her eyes became huge and her chin almost dropped to the floor. She was speechless and staring at me. Finally, she spoke. "How did you know all this?"

I said, "Let me tell you what else I know about this Chemtool company. I know they generated a lot of hazardous waste such as oils and solvents. I also know that the company had to dispose of those hazardous materials and hired another company to do so for approximately 25 years. And when you bought out this company, you kicked out the company that was getting rid of the hazardous waste, even though they had a 25-year relationship with Chemtool. And that's when the fire started right after you took over. Almost like karma."

She looked at me and said, "Who are you? How do you know all these things?"

I replied, "Let me explain how I know these things. You see, I'm retired and my company is a precious metal refinery, but we also have a division that does hazardous waste materials disposal. My company had been doing the disposal of that hazardous waste until you bought them out and got rid of us. Then you had the fire." Kiddingly, I added, "Ya see, it serves you right for dropping us as your vendor."

"So let me understand this," she said. "You are the owner of the company from which my company took away all the hazardous waste business?"

"Yes," I replied, "you're speaking with the owner."

She said, "This really is weird. I'm the one who took it away from you!"

Really, what are the odds of me being in a pharmacy over 7,700 miles away from a town in Illinois, where I don't even live anymore, and you happen to be nice enough to overhear an American having difficulty with a translation of Portuguese into English. You are standing right next to me! You could've been one aisle over, and we never would've met. How did that happen?

ISN'T THAT WEIRD!

And now it gets a little more bizarre as signs from the universe go both ways. Not only did I need help, but she was also in need of some information from the universe, through me. My need for some translation was immediate. She needed something not as pressing, but it was something she had been thinking about.

Let me back up a few moments, to just after we both said, "How amazing is this coincidence?" The woman asked us both who we really were, and what we were doing there.

In order to dispel her belief that we were some kind of secret agents tracking her, I explained that both Jamie and I were retired, that we lived in Hawaii for at least six months of the year, and the other months we traveled—sometimes domestically, but mostly out of the country. I told her we were lovers of life and adventure, that we loved scuba diving, and tried to do it wherever we went.

"Oh my God," she said, "I can't believe you love scuba diving! That's one of my passions; my father and I dive all the time, but he's 80 years old now and getting a little tired. I hope I can at least fulfill my bucket list before he's no longer available to go diving with me."

"What's on your bucket list?" I asked. "Where do you want to go before you stop diving with him?

"There's only one place a scuba diver wants to go," she said, "and you know it. It's the Maldives."

Now it was getting even weirder.

I said "OK, take a breath and listen to my story about the Maldives. As

I said, we live in Hawaii for half the year and travel the rest of the year. Of course, until recently, perhaps a year ago, I thought the best place to dive was Hawaii, with its beautiful corals—just paradise! How could there be a better place to dive than Hawaii?"

It was almost on cue: When I said I agreed with her about the Maldives being on every scuba diver's bucket list, if someone had been watching the both of us, they would've thought we were two attendees at a trade show of mouth droppers (lol).

She said, "My father is getting too old to go with me, and as much as I want to go to the Maldives, I just don't know where to go, as there are 1200 little islands, of which only 200 are inhabited. And then I'm supposed to find a dive shop—an unbelievable task."

Once again, I started to smile.

"What do you know now?" she said. "You are unbelievable!"

Again on cue, mouths dropped as if we were saying "Ahhhhh" in a dental chair, and we all laughed. "OK, Miss Brazil," I said, "sit back and let me tell you what I know about the Maldives." By this time, we had left the pharmacy together and were sitting in the rest area of the mall sipping coffee. I told her to relax as I had another story to tell her.

After Jamie and I had been dating for less than a year, I introduced her to the world of scuba diving, where there are two requirements to get certified as a diver. In fact, you must do these two things to become certified: take classes and go into a swimming pool to try out the skills you learned in class. These skills are required to be a proficient scuba diver, and they have to be practiced before you go into the ocean. I had originally been certified in the Chicago area by a company called the Frog Pond Dive Shop, but unfortunately due to COVID, they went out of business. So, there I was in Illinois, not knowing whom to call, where to go, or what scuba shop I should use. Now listen to my story and watch this all unfold; afterward, I want you to tell me if there is a universe that watches over us all or at least puts the parts together for us to choose.

I googled it and found a scuba shop within 15 minutes of where I was at the time. I called and told them my girlfriend was interested in scuba, that I was already certified, and could I come in and speak with them? So, I drove over to their shop and met Nick, the owner of Berry Scuba in Northfield, Illinois. I explained to him what I wanted to do, and he said, "Of course." I also told him that it had been a while since I had dived, and that I could use a recertification in the pool as well. "No problem," he said. "Let me introduce you to the gentleman who does the certification for the pool; his name is Mujay."

Of course, that was an interesting name, and you can probably guess where he was from: yes, you got it! The Maldives. Mujay worked only part-time at Berry Scuba, and I was lucky to have met him on a day he was there. How weird that we caught him when he was available!

We went through the certification for the pool with Mujay, and Jamie and I became close friends with him. In fact, we became so close he invited us out to the Maldives, told us when he was going to be there, and although you don't know us that well, I can tell you that's all it took for Jamie and I to decide where we were going next. And to the Maldives we did go, but only after Jamie received her open- water certification for diving back in Hawaii.

In fact, just as a side note, the only reason I agreed to go to India with Jamie was that it only looked to be about two or three inches on the map between India and the Maldives. Thus, the trip was planned. In reality, it took almost five and a half hours to get to the Maldives from India! We are kind of impetuous and impulsive.

OK, so follow all these parts of the story. This is amazing, even to me, and I have a leading role in the storyline. There are many, many dive shops in the Chicagoland area. Many. I picked a place called Berry Dive Shop in Northfield, Illinois, just less than 15 minutes from where I was. Lucky? Keep reading. So, I introduced myself to the owner of the dive shop. As I said, I told Nick, the owner, that my old dive shop had closed, but I wanted to introduce my fiancée to scuba. I asked if he knew of a dive shop for learning the skills in a pool. Many dive shops do not have their own pool.

"Of course," he said. "We have a pool right here (weird again), and in three days the next in-house classroom will be starting." Of course we signed Jamie up, and in three days, she was doing the classroom lessons and getting ready for her pool certification.

She nailed the classroom stuff, and into the pool we went. We both went, as I needed a refresher course, so what the hell. We were introduced to the dive master Mujay, a small man with shoulder-length salt and pepper hair. The dark-skinned Maldivian fellow had no fat, a big smile, and 10,000 dives under his belt—a perfect diving instructor! In this scuba game, the weirder the better and this guy looked weird, but weird is what happened next.

Jamie passed the classroom and pool tests, got her pool certification, and then we went back to Hawaii for her open water certification, which she did flawlessly. So now Jamie was a PADI-certified open water diver. Yay for Jamie! Oh yeah, the weird part.

Jamie and I went diving with Mujay's operation along with his lovely wife Arnavas. We stayed in a luxurious penthouse in the Maldives, had dinner at Mujay's home with his family, and dove with the best group of people ever. We went back again in October 2023, and dove off a 150-foot live-aboard boat for 10 days, on which we had our own stateroom. Mujáy and Arnavas have become such good friends of ours that they were invited to our wedding party. (More about the wedding party later.)

Now that's fucking weird!

Life does move in mysterious ways, doesn't it? But the point here is that you must be open to the universe to receive these signs and messages. It really does work; I swear it does! All right, campers, let's move on with this stream of consciousness. I thought I would have to write down all these experiences lest I forget them, but that is not the case. Nope, no need to remember, as every damn day, EVERY DAY, there is something new and weird happening. I get tired of trying to remember them all. But there is no reason to remember old things, as new things happen all the time. I noted a few of them so I could share them with you as I write this book, so I don't think I'm jumping around without purpose. I do have purpose, but yes, I am jumping around!

Lesson to learn:

Life is amazing. It truly is. The universe is out there watching us, watching every move we make and trying to connect with us through signs and signals. It doesn't matter what you think; I'm telling you from my experience. These things are real and these things actually happen. Don't be avoidant of signs and signals. They are out there for a reason. The universe loves you and only wants the best for you, but you've got to join in to play the game. Make your own decisions when you see happenings that make you step back for a moment or grab your breath. There's a reason for that. It's a combination. It's your feelings, your signs from the universe, and somehow, you are being told by the universe about doing something or not doing something. It is absolutely magical and amazing that these things happen, and they do.

REALLY, THEY DO.

CHAPTER SEVEN

Wake Up, People

So, if you're sharp, you're already thinking to yourself, *How can I be asleep if I'm reading this?* Well, Sparky, you might be astute and breathing, but it doesn't mean you're not going through your daily activities asleep. The world is full of people who arise at 6 a.m., leave for work at 7 a.m., arrive at work and stay till 5 p.m. with, of course, their lunch at noon. Then they drive home to arrive there by 6 p.m. Sometimes, their days are so boring they don't remember the drive home. Rang a bell, didn't it?

They are metaphorically asleep, comatose, zombies, whatever you wish to call it. Life isn't a dress rehearsal. This is real shit. They shoot real bullets out there in reality land. Wake up people, it happens. As corny as it sounds, yesterday is gone, tomorrow isn't promised to anybody, and perhaps the present is called the "present" because it is a gift, so don't waste time. I don't care how rich you are; you can't buy more time.

Remember COVID? I was asleep as well. Not long ago, I was a dazed sheep, just moving around. I took those vaccines, two and a booster. Yeah, and a gift from Big Pharma of A-fib. It happens. How did I allow that to happen to me? You must question everything. How can you not? When I was growing up in the '60s, they said to trust no one over 30, and they were right. Don't agree to agree or agree to do something just to fit in. Don't agree so as to not make waves. Rather, ask questions and upset the norm, the standards, and whatever else we are told is acceptable because "they told us it was 'right' for us." Remember taking the road less traveled? A-fib was my wake-up call; no more just going along with the norm. The road less traveled is my route of choice. My life has been all the better because of that road, and I'm not telling anybody about my shortcut because I like the traffic pattern right now—not too many of us out there with our heads clear, focused, and determined. The traffic is light.

I think that's what I'm trying to tell you. *Carpe diem*—seize the day. Enjoy the moment because nothing, and I mean nothing, lasts forever. And if you're strong enough, then do yourself a favor. When times suck, savor the suck. Just feel how bad things are, and try to remember this terrible time, because as sure as shit, things will improve if you're pumping blood. And then when you're feeling good, reflect on those shitty times and the feeling of how good things are now, and it will be all the sweeter. Savor the good AND the bad times, and you will enjoy the future all the more. You will look back on yourself and think about when you thought the world was coming to an end, but it didn't. Somehow you got through those terrible times, and how sweet it seems today, only because it is.

You've got to experience the depths of misery before you can ever enjoy all the good that lies before you. I think it was Richard Nixon who said, "You can't appreciate the beauty from the top of the mountain unless you've been in the valley of darkness."

Don't just stumble through life; stand up and do something about it. If you don't like where you are, then do something about that. Change your perspective and you change your reality. There is no absolute truth. Life is how we view it. We aren't right or wrong. We are just here and now. This is it. It doesn't get any better or worse unless we deem it so. I know that when we give something a lot of attention, it becomes a lot more important. Things we give a lot of attention to expand. If you want something, then *do* something because nothing happens to us without effort, and it's up to us.

Like Nike says, Just Do It! (Oh, and if I woke you, I'm sorry. Go back to sleep.) It's all up to you, so rise and shine, Sparky. The future is yours, so make it happen. As much as I hate to say it, nobody cares about your life more than you. Remember *carpe diem* and what it takes to seize the day, because once that day is gone, it's gone! There is no change without change.

Lesson to learn:

If you really want to enjoy your life, then you have to experience it. So many of us are just knee-deep in the water and go no further because we either don't know how to swim or don't know where to swim. People like this want the water nice and warm without any waves so they can just be comfortable. Comfortable ain't gonna get it for you, Carl.

Have you ever jumped into a pool of cold water? How did you feel? I'm sure it got your attention, but didn't it make you feel alive? The point I'm making is that you've got to have some discomfort, and you've got to be strong enough to be apart from everyone else. Don't look for approval, as you're not going to get it. The popular way is not the only way to think of what you want; think of the goals you have, and then do what no one else is willing to do: fight your ass off to get what you want, even if everyone is against you, even if no one gives you approval. Just do it. Don't look for approval from everybody else; look into yourself, and if you can look in that mirror and know you've taken the road less traveled, you will be so much the better for it. It takes guts, dedication, perseverance, and confidence. Just do it.

Remember, there are only three kinds of people in this world: those who make things happen, those who watch things happen, and those who say, "What happened?"

It's your choice. Pick one.

NOW.

CHAPTER EIGHT

The Girl with the Prosthetic Leg

So, in the last chapter, I told you that I was in Curitiba, Brazil. What a beautiful city! It was designed by the famous architect Jaimie Lerner and later governed by him as the mayor. This is a world-class city. Recently chosen for the "number one smart city in the world" award, it is clean and kind, yet international, and an oasis in comparison to most cities. Jamie and I were given a tour of the city by a friend of ours named Juan Carlos. He took us to the parks and the rainforest and showed us the beauty of the city, which appeared to be on steroids. The tour included so much more, and it seemed as if Jaimie Lerner himself, architect and mayor of Curitiba, was our tour guide. That really was almost possible, because Juan was next-door neighbor to Mr. Lerner and knew him extremely well before his passing. Because of the unique insights our friend had through knowing Jaimie Lerner, we were able to go to special places that most tourists never see.

Juan Carlos took us to a secluded area deep within a mini-rainforest. As we entered the rainforest, we walked down a path that was perhaps only six feet wide and covered by the most magnificent foliage we had ever seen, almost like a canopy. It got darker and darker. After a few minutes, we saw a light at the end of our path. Gradually, the rainforest started to grow brighter and the darkness diminished. As we approached the exit, we were shown an entire vision, to say the least. I don't know if I have the correct words to express the immensity, the enormity, and the beauty that stood before us. A huge and imposing mountain of chiseled black rock towered so high you could not see its top. In front of this imposing, intimidating, and dwarfing mountain of black stone was the most beautiful pool that stretched out before us. The color of the water was enhanced by the sun peeking out from all sides of this monument. I remember seeing the most beautiful turquoise water ever. I don't have the words to justify it, but I'm sure you have seen pictures of the Caribbean with its turquoise blue waters. This was better. I mean, a sight that takes your breath away; a sight that makes you gasp. This was our view, and on this pond were ducks and swans—white ones and black ones. The black rock before us was as handsome and rugged as nature can present, and the colors of the shimmering pool against the beauty of nature's creatures were a sight I will never forget.

I think if I had to prove that God exists, then this would be the place to show proof so perfect, so raw, and so inspiring. Several benches lined the shoreline, and the bench on my left was vacant. The bench on my right was occupied by a demure young lady. I remember noticing her when we arrived. This was a true place of God. I even found myself whispering when we spoke, and I thought to myself that it was almost like being in a church. So, now you have the scene. A beautiful place, serene, and yet at the same time also spiritual and Godlike. There was no sound . . . the place seemed eerily quiet, as if I were walking into a library. I felt small, as if I were only a speck in the scenery. I viewed my presence there as unimportant, only an incidental adjunct to the scene.

All was serene, spiritual, and Godlike, and then reality appeared as the young girl, who was sitting on the park bench alone, got up and decided to walk by me to exit. She was young, angelic, sweet, and well-dressed from head to toe . . . and then I noticed her leg. It was made of metal, and I realized that within this beauty, the universe wanted to remind me that no matter how serene and beautiful the moment might be in this world, we must enjoy it. We must savor it and embrace it. The reality of life came right off that park bench the young girl was sitting on. I guess what I'm trying to convey to everyone is that life is tough. The world can be raw and ugly. Life is not easy, nor is it always pretty. There is a lesson within all this, and I believe it is no matter how pleasant a moment may be, we all have to be smart enough to enjoy it, to *carpe diem* if you will—seize the day, the moment that is so great UNTIL IT'S NOT!

That's right. Everything has a term, a moment, a finite moment. Confused? Let me clarify for you.

Lesson to learn:

This is another variation of *carpe diem*. And while this means to seize the day, there is a reason for it. When you come upon something beautiful, when you come upon something special, upon anything that gives you peace, comfort, and enjoyment, just remember to seize those moments. Those good moments that we all enjoy are important for two reasons: because they feel good, and for another reason that nobody really thinks about—it sets us up for the present feeling of enjoying that beauty because we know nothing lasts forever. Bad things will happen, and bad things always do. It's the way the world works. You can't relish the heights of enjoyment and beauty if you haven't been to the depths of darkness. Do not take these moments for granted. Stay in the moment. Enjoy the feeling and let your senses explore and receive. Always remember that no matter what, nothing stays static. Everything changes, even when things are terrible. It won't stay that way forever. Sometimes it'll get worse. But more often than not, if we're hitting the bottom, it won't last forever so enjoy it. I'm not telling you to be a pessimist. I'm saying, be a realist.

I'm just saying....

CHAPTER NINE

Everything and Everyone Has a Term Limit
Except Members of Congress

Everything is great until it's not. My health is great until it's not. The market keeps going up until it goes down. I love my job until I don't! Do you get the idea Sparky? Nothing lasts forever. It's just the way life goes: good and bad. Think about this. In fact, re-read this paragraph if you don't get it, but there is a good side to all of this.

My life is shit until it's not (just follow the bouncing ball, Bob-O). I'm miserable in my marriage until I decide to get a divorce. Then life changes. Yes, it was miserable, and then during the divorce, it didn't get better. It got fucking worse! But wait, there's more.

Yes, it went from bad to miserable; but remember, even bad ends. However, don't get cocky. It went from a bad marriage to a miserable divorce. I told you nothing lasts forever, but the miserable divorce allowed me to get to a much better life: meeting a wonderful woman, exploring new adventures, having fun, traveling, meeting new friends, and loving life. So, no matter where life leads you, from good to bad, to worse or whatever, enjoy the ride and smile at the bad stuff so you can laugh and enjoy the good stuff. Let's take this to the universal law that affects us all, with no exceptions.

Got your attention, didn't I?

Lesson to learn:

Life is about moments. When we go on vacation, what are we doing? We are going for a week or two weeks, so there is a finite period of time. The good times we have on vacation are balanced out when we have to go home to reality. It doesn't always have to reach the heights of ecstasy and then fall to the depths of depravity. There is moderation in life. The main point is that you must be aware of the moment that you are enjoying. Another way, of course, is to just stay in the moment, stay in the present, and open your eyes and ears to enjoy it. Save it and embrace it because before you know it, Sparky, you're back home into reality, which isn't the most terrible thing but it sure isn't as good as a vacation. You get the point, Peter? Life and experiences are never static. It's like the weather in Chicago—if you don't like it, wait 10 minutes because it's sure to change. Short chapter, easy lesson to understand.

CHAPTER TEN

The Universal Law

This law applies to everyone reading this. This law applies to everyone *not* reading this. This law applies to everyone who is . . . did I say, to EVERYONE? EVERYONE! NO EXCEPTIONS.

Here is the deal. We all want the good stuff in life. I want a fancy car. I want a good grade on the test. I want to lose 20 pounds. I want the pretty girl with me. I want to be rich. See the trend yet, Willis?

We all want things—stuff that's material and stuff that's not. We're human and that's how we roll. So how do we get them? That's where the universal law sets in. Do you want a nice car? You've got to work your ass off at whatever you do, hard and long, in order to get the money to buy the car. Grades on a test? Study your ass off. Lose 20 pounds? Diet, exercise, cut back, and eat healthy. Pretty girl? Pursue her, woo her, work at the relationship, and make her feel like the most important girl in the world. Rich? If it's screwing people out of money, working for the man, a job, a corporation, or begging, get your ass moving because no one is going to give you anything just because you're pretty . . . get it, Gloria? The ONLY WAY to *get* the good stuff in life is to go and *do* the hard stuff and *work* through the tough stuff, because the good stuff is what you get when you finish the hard stuff. Did you follow that?

I almost forgot a small issue: Doing the hard stuff is work; it hurts, it's tiring, it is not fun. Maybe that's why they call it "work" and not "fun." Nevertheless, without the work, the anguish, the pain, and the sweat, the next step would not be as sweet as it is.

That's why it is so sweet when you get something accomplished. You did the hard stuff because that's the only route to get to the good stuff. I don't know how much simpler I can make this for you. If you try to fool the system and do not do the work, here is what happens:

Wanted the car? Didn't work at your job, so no money and no car. Wanted a good test grade? Didn't study, so then you're stupid, and guess what—you get an F. Congratulations, stupid. Wanted to lose that 20 pounds? Didn't want to diet and work out because you know better, but ha ha, you're still fat. You get the idea, don't you?

NO EXCEPTIONS - NO EXCUSES

This law works because this IS the universal law of life. End of discussion. And it applies to all of us, even if you refuse to recognize the law. Tag, you're it.

Lesson to learn:

Even Ray Charles can see how this law operates. It can be something as simple as getting along with your significant other—if you want to have good times with that person, then you've got to communicate and work out any difficulties that you have. And this isn't something I should have to show all of you out there. This is something you're living every single day if you're honest and aware. And what I mean by honest is, do you have enough of a backbone and enough control over your ego to recognize the only things you've ever achieved in your life that are worthy and good are those you have worked for? It's really as simple as that. You reap what you sow. The rule still holds true: If you want something, you have to work for it; there's just no way around it. End of story. I wish it was easier. I wish there was someone you could bribe, but it never seems to work. As we say, it is what it is.

CHAPTER ELEVEN

What's Your Perspective?

At this place in the book, you're possibly thinking, *Wow, this guy is weird himself. He looks at things so differently, but why? He seems to find humor in almost every situation. He must love Seinfeld.*

He does, and I do. And don't think I never think Larry David and I have lots in common, because we do.

So, here is a raw example of how I view things. It's not right or wrong; it is what it is. Most important is that it's my way of looking at life. Don't flinch. You don't have to think like me. You just have to think like you. It's called perspective. *Your* perspective. If you don't like it, you can change it. That's how we always change our reality. If you're not happy where you're at, change the way you are looking at things—change your perspective. It's that simple. A friend of mine, a young girl, related a story to me. Her parents had died a few years before in a horrific car accident and for some reason—memories or laziness—she and her sister held onto the family home. Now it was time to sell the home after three years, as it was getting too expensive to maintain.

The sisters went up to the proverbial attic to clean and prepare for the sale. Looking through some boxes of this and that, they came upon a box of photographs. There were stacks and stacks of Polaroid pictures from the old days, and while looking through the box, one of the sisters came upon a few pictures that surprised her. On several of them, she was shocked to view both their mom and dad engaging in sexual activities with each other. She could tell by looking at the pictures that her mom was a true animal lover as she really loved her doggy position. My friend told me that both she and her sister were aghast by the photos. How could their parents do that, she wondered.

I laughed and said she shouldn't have asked how they could do that; the more appropriate question should be who took the pictures? Perspective.

Ha, ha, ha, life certainly is weird.

Lesson to learn:

As the chapter says, it's all about how you look at things as everybody sees things from their own perspective. Actually, this is a life-saving lesson to learn. Think about it: you're depressed, you're miserable. Life sucks and all you do is mope around with your head down and shoulders hunched. You are unhappy, so what can you do? Of course, you can get a shrink, a counselor, a therapist, or whomever, and you can pour your heart out to them. And all they do is listen and then charge for it. There's a simpler way, but don't get me wrong. I understand there are people with severe psychological problems who need professional help. I'm not talking about them. I'm talking about the everyday depression and moping and misery that some of us, even I, have experienced from time to time. This lesson will save you time, money, and aggravation: another bargain for buying my book.

Remember, no two emotions can be shared at the same time, nor can activities. It seems like 100 years ago that I was sent to overnight camp at age 10 to help me become independent. . So, what did I do? As much as I hate to admit it, I felt homesick. When no one was around, I sat in my tent whenever I could and cried into my pillow. I missed Mommy, Daddy, and my home. I was unhappy. I thought I was alone in the area where we slept while everyone else was at some activity. Looking back, I realize I was fortunate that a counselor walked by and heard me sobbing into my pillow.

This counselor was a kind, older fellow. He sat on my bunk and said, "Hey kid, let me give you a clue. You can't be homesick and happy at the same time, so what do you need to do here? Get active, change what you're doing, get out of this bed, get going, and do something else. You watch—all of a sudden, you'll realize you're not homesick after all."

He was right of course. I didn't know about perspective then, and I probably wouldn't have understood what that meant, but the lesson was true when I was 10 years old, and it's true at 78. If you're not happy with the situation, or the people you're around, or whatever it is you're doing, snap out of it, Sparky. If you don't like the way things are, just change your perspective and it'll change your reality. This is a constant theme throughout this book and a lesson I had to learn the hard way. Do this for yourself and you will have a wonderful day in spite of whatever has gone wrong. It's just a neat little way to avoid the couch at the psychiatrist's office and save some money.

Here's the deal: it's really quick. There is no right and there is no wrong. There is only your right or wrong, my right or wrong, his right or wrong. Do you see where the train is going, Timmy? But none of us realize this, and we argue and bicker and fight with our neighbors and friends and other countries over politics. It's all so simple. We just need moderation, but that's another story for later.

CHAPTER TWELVE

Sailing Down the River of Life

What truly is perspective? You and I, he and she—we all look at things differently, even if all four of us look at one thing, let's say something as simple as a pen on a table. Ask all four of us about the pen and you will get four different descriptions. It's called perspective. Now let me make this more graphic for you.

Forget about your current life. Instead, imagine if you will that each and every one of us is in our own 55-gallon open-top drum, drifting in the sea of life. We live in it, we dine in it, and we even shit in it. Yes, we live with our own shit. It's our shit from our life, from our experiences and from the way we were raised. So, what we do determines the quality and the quantity of our own shit. There we are, each watching from near to far: we watch our neighbors, friends, and unknowns who are all awash in a sea of 55-gallon drums, floating down the river of life, each with our own shit and our combined stench (like when I asked a cab driver, when visiting New York for the first time, what that smell was, and he said, "Brooklyn.") And on and on we float.

Remember, humans are social animals; we just don't like to keep to ourselves. We engage others in conversation and as human nature goes, we love to make sure that the grass that appears greener in the other drums we watch float by is better or worse than our grass. We may make contact with someone else as they're floating down the river of life in their own 55-gallon drum, and here is how contagion of crap occurs in the real world.

We identify or select someone in their specific 55-gallon drum, and what do we do first? Once the decision has been made to join somebody else in their drum—which always looks, at first blush, to be a better situation than ours—we decide to take the leap and join them. Now, here is where we must watch the concept of contamination and cross-contamination. When we leave our 55-gallon drum, we of course leave the majority of our shit in our former drum. Yes, that's true, but there is always some shit we carry over into the new drum. Not only have we entered the new drum with some of our shit clinging to us, but we have created a new blend of shit called OUR shit. Understand that deciding to join a new drum holds a lot of possibilities. We could be joining a drum for a romantic event, a new job, a new friendship, a new place to be, a new whatever—it's new Nancy but it's still shit. At least it's new shit or different shit, so that's a little bit different and offers a slightly different perspective than what we are now enjoying. As I mentioned, it's called NEW SHIT or OUR SHIT.

A phenomenon happens in the new drum we enter. While it's a new drum to us, it's still a bunch of shit that was and is a continuously evolving drum of crap on its way down the river before we got there . . . think of it as a soap opera continuum.

It might be a *General Hospital* script, but the question we have to ask ourselves is, "After 30 years of TV drama, is it Luke's baby?" The point is that once you enter a new drum, you are literally—and remember this, folks— without a choice, continuing with the drama that is and was going on in that drum before your appearance. Like I said, it is a new blend of shit that we live with, and also a new perspective resulting from this change of drum residence.

So, here's the point of this discussion about perspective from old drums, present drums, and drums yet to be selected. Whether you're in an old drum or a new drum, your perspective is your reality. If you're not happy with your reality in your new drum or old drum, then all you have to do is change your perspective and then you will have a new reality. And you don't even have to move from your present drum. But if you're really miserable with the perspective/reality of your job, your marriage, etc., then you always have the choice to abandon your shit, or your drum, to be more specific.

You'll have a new perspective, a new reality, and that my friends is how perspective and reality are constantly changing and ever evolving. We determine whether to stay in our wonderful or miserable drums by pleasure or pain. Yes, pleasure and pain—an interesting concept. Let me digress if you will.

In August 2011, way before I knew about the universe and the signs or messages from whomever, my business required me to travel two weeks per month for a week at a time, for two reasons. The first reason: I was expanding my business nationwide by calling on printers for lithographic films and scrap, so I could continue on with the recovery from their materials and their film processors. The second reason: After the last 30 to 40 years of marriage, I realized I was done living a lie. My marriage sucked; I was absolutely miserable and emotionally bankrupt. Traveling became my vacations from the marriage, and I was emotionally shut down from my wife. My new mistress was work. I'm not proud of it; it cost me big-time, financially and emotionally.

I buried the thought of eventually getting a divorce. It scared me. It plagued me. It rocked my world, so I buried it deep and continued on.

Lesson to learn:

Don't be scared, little man. Mommy is here for you, sugarplum. Really, Ralph? I don't think so. No, that's not the way it works. It comes down to this: It is what it is—no more, and I promise you no less than it actually is, or what you perceive your truth to be.

You see, we all think our world is everything, and in a way it is. It's not only everything. It's the only thing. It's our perspective. It's our viewpoint. It's our look at the world and whom we're floating around with, or perhaps it's solo, but nevertheless it's ours.

Everybody thinks everybody else is better than us, less than us, equal to us, or at least different than us, and the truth of the matter is that we are all the same, and only a little different. The point I'm trying to make is that none of us, from the President to the pooper scooper, are any better than anyone else. We wear different clothing perhaps, and have different skin colors, but basically, we're all the same. We are all just trying to get home. We all just want to feed our families. We all just want comfort and caring, but we sure complicate the shit out of it.

CHAPTER THIRTEEN

The Universe Was Waiting for Me at the Airport

Back to the airplane for more business travel. I traveled so much that I had to check my ticket to see what city I was either going to or coming from. Onto the next flight. I plopped down into my first-class seat, as I was making good money, and sat next to some guy . . . but excuse me; I got ahead of myself. Let me back up to an hour before the flight.

Before getting on the plane, I wandered around the airport seeking something to occupy my time while on the flight. I went into a bookstore and looked for something to get lost in. Nothing obvious. The closest thing that interested me was a book entitled, *How to Make Tough Decisions Through Pleasure and Pain*. So, I bought the book, stuffed it in my backpack, and headed to the gate. More about that book later. (Remember, I didn't know about the universe or signs. That insight came later.)

Back to my airplane experience with the universe. The guy next to me was just a guy. We nodded to each other but said nothing. After we took off and had our free peanuts delivered, he turned to me and said, "What the hell is your problem? Maybe I can help you."

What the fuck! Was I getting into a fight over nothing or did say he wanted to help me? I responded to him, "What are you talking about?"

He said to me, "You obviously have a problem. I can feel it. What's going on with you?"

I felt like a deer stuck in headlights. We talked about love, marriage, divorce, and kids. The three-hour flight was over, and it seemed like 15 minutes had gone by. We exchanged business cards and have been corresponding for over 25 years. Only now do I realize that he was sent to me as a sign from the universe. By the way, he says hello, as I told him about this book and that he is in it.

The world is amazing. If you're willing to receive it, I introduce to you a gentleman by the name of Jeff Dana. I couldn't identify him visually if you asked me, because it's been so many years since we met, but every so often I'll call him up and we'll discuss where we both are in our lives.

OK, I owe you all an apology. It's been months since I journaled. Since this book is about stream of consciousness, it won't matter where we continue. Sorry if it seems like I'm jumping around, but I am. Deal with it.

Lesson to learn:

There is a reason that I met Jeff. I needed him, his wisdom and experiences. He helped me sort out things. He had gone through similar life experiences and had to make me realized that I was not alone. Thanks Jeff, I needed you, I appreciate you and I want all of you to know out there that there are good people in the world waiting to meet you as well. Its a good world out there with good stories and experiences. All you need to do is leave the door open for them and be honest and truthful. So just let me say, thanks Jeff Dana for making a difference in my life's journey.

CHAPTER FOURTEEN

The Wedding and Gratitude Party

Let's go to the start of 2023. Happy New Year to all. Remember, Jamie and I decided to get married, but where in the world would we do it? Jamie comes from the Pacific Northwest and I'm from Chicago. We live half the year in Hawaii and the other half of the year, we travel quite a bit. We couldn't expect people to fly to Hawaii. Jamie and I had both lived in the center of the country; she lived in Hinsdale, Illinois for 25 years and I, of course, lived my whole life in Chicago. So, what could we do? The Pacific Northwest was too damn cold, and Hawaii was too damn far and expensive for people to go to.

Since Jamie and I had both been married before, this wasn't our first rodeo, and because we're older, we also realized that getting married late in life was a personal decision that would only affect Jamie and me. So, we decided to split the difference. We decided to make ourselves happy. There is a beautiful hotel, an absolutely fabulous one, called the Mauna Lani here on the island of Hawaii. We invited Jamie's cousin and her husband to dinner and set up a dinner date for her cousins and another couple, to make it a surprise wedding. We held a very intimate wedding for just the two of us at the Mauna Lani. It was fabulous, everything Jamie and I wanted, and all without anybody's opinion of what we were doing. It was great.

We had four guests, and with the two of us, a total of six. It was absolutely beautiful and more than either of us ever expected. It was perfect.

Now I must digress a bit, because not everybody was as happy for us to get married as we had hoped; you know how family works. That's why we decided to keep the wedding private and not tell anybody about it until some other things had calmed down. We decided that we would go to Chicago and make our announcement when things were right.

Again, I have to digress because, by the time we got married, Jamie and I had lost a few people. Jamie had an employee from her company who was like family—a young man, a widower, who was caring for his six-year-old son. Unfortunately, one night at 2 a.m., due to bad weather he had a bad traffic accident and was killed, leaving his son an orphan. I myself had a good friend named Mark Hofstein, whom I spoke to quite frequently as he lived in St. Louis and I lived in Chicago. We went to college together and had been fast friends since our freshman year. One day, I received a call from his wife Roz who said "Shelly, Mark is sick. I don't know what to do."

I told her, "Please get him to the doctor and let's check him out." Mark was not responsive when he woke up on Monday morning. He went to the hospital for tests, was admitted to the hospital on Wednesday, and was dead by Friday. Shocking, just shocking.

Jamie and I both knew in our hearts that life is short and that the people we care about and love are only loaned to us. We have to take the moment to tell people how much we love and care about them while we can, because when it's too late, it's just that . . . too late.

Jamie came up with a great idea. Why don't we have a gratitude party? "A gratitude party?" I asked. "What is that?"

"You know," she replied, "It's a party to which we invite people who have made a difference or had a positive influence in our lives, and people we love and care about. The *real* people—the ones who really make a difference in our lives and the ones that count."

OK, there will be more about the gratitude party, but first (and I know I'm jumping around but that's how I do it) I've got to tell you about the wedding. It was great, and like I told you, it was going to be a surprise wedding, but right before the evening started, maybe an hour or two before we were supposed to all be at the so-called "dinner," we received a phone call from Jamie's cousin stating that her husband's back was killing him and he couldn't make it for dinner. She said, "Sorry about that," and wondered if we could pick up the other guests and bring them out for the dinner.

We were nowhere near where the other guests were, and Jamie just couldn't keep the surprise anymore. She said, "Cousin, get your ass to the dinner now because we're getting married tonight. It's our wedding, so tell your husband two things: one is that we're getting married tonight so that's the main course, and two, tell him to take an extra pain pill and get his ass to a wedding . . . *our* wedding! And show up they did, of course, along with the other couple who had no idea where the hell they were or what the hell we were doing. Nevertheless, all six of us were together, and it was great.

I've been to a lot of weddings in my day, but I have to say it was really fabulous—a traditional Jewish wedding with a Shiksa bride, which means she is not Jewish. Jamie was beautiful and still is; for once in my life, I listened to the universe, and this felt so right because it was. And I am more in love today than when I met her. I am blessed. Truly blessed. We didn't tell anyone that we got married. Imagine all this planning and secrecy of a wedding and marriage from a guy who said he'd never get married again, and when I say never ever, I mean *never ever*. So, be careful. You never know when you're going to be eating your words, but how sweet the result.

Like I said, we told no one for a couple of reasons. The first reason was family members. Some may not have been happy for us, but plenty would have liked to share their negative opinions, and we weren't really interested in listening to anybody. The other reason we didn't tell anybody was that we weren't interested in people's judgments. So, we just enjoyed the wedding, took pictures, had a beautiful violin play for us, and made our memories.

So, fast forward to after the wedding. Remember, we were planning a gratitude party for those who have had a positive influence on our lives. At the end of the party, we planned to show pictures of the wedding and announce to all that we really were married.

Chicago made sense for the party. We booked the venue at a friend of mine's country club, and a party was made. We hired a DJ, a photographer, and a florist, and picked out the best they had to offer in food, an open bar, handouts, Hawaii themes, and party favors. We made the whole party have a touch of Hawaii, as everyone knew it was where we were living. We had tropical drinks, Hawaiian leis, and even a picture booth to retain the memories. The best part of the evening was the start of the party and the introduction to everyone. You have to understand that people thought they were coming to a wedding. They all thought they were smarter than us, so here's what happened:

I grabbed the microphone from the DJ and said to all, "Hey guys, everybody is here for a reason, and for those from Jamie's side who don't know me, I'm Shelly, and from those of you from my side who don't know Jamie, she's Jamie!"

Simple enough.

"Let me get rid of one illusion that I'm sure a lot of you have, because I've been deflecting a lot of comments from some of you. Jamie and I are not getting married tonight. There is no wedding here tonight. Nope, no wedding at all."

They all looked at me like deer in headlights. "Then why are we here?"

I heard someone ask.

I went on, "Whether you realize it or not, I said you are all here for a reason. And the reason is that you have had, in some way, whether it be small or large, a positive influence on both of our lives: Jamie's life, my life, and our life together. That's why you are here—because Jamie and I love you. No more, no less. But all of you must realize that all of us have lost loved ones—friends, family, and whoever—have passed and cannot be here this evening. Perhaps the deaths were sudden, or from illness or accident. Whatever the cause, one thing is true, people. That person is gone. That person is never going to return to this life. They are nothing but a memory right now. Do you have regrets? Did you wish you had more time? (We all think we always have more time.) It's true that we don't know how long we have, but we certainly know the heartache of not having been able to say, "We love you," "We care about you," or "We want you in our lives" while they are alive rather than when they're dead and it's just too late."

I continued, "And when you reflect back on the memory of those people who are gone, was there something you wish you could've said, something you wanted them to know—that you loved them, that you valued their opinion and their approval, or just that you valued them as a good friend?

"If you didn't get that chance to tell your loved ones and friends how you felt, that's sad, and it's too bad. Listen, I told you all that Jamie and I selected each and every one of you here because you are special to us. We love you, we care about you, and in some way, you made us both better people. So, we say to all of you, thank you and we love you, now, while you're here, while you're alive, while you can hear our words.

"Now, I must ask all of you a favor. You all came here with someone: a spouse, a mother, a friend, a husband, a wife . . . someone special to you to share this evening with. So, for the next 60 seconds, for just one minute, I want you to turn to that person, hold their hands, look them in their eyes, and tell them with all honesty and real emotion how you feel about them. Do this before it's too late, right here and now. Let them know, with all emotions open, and no ego or false pride. This is the time, and you'll never have another moment like this one."

With that, I shut my mouth and for 60 seconds watched people turn to each other and hold hands. I watched people tear up. The tears fell, and the hugging was beautiful.

I guess that's all it took because as I mentioned, the tears flowed and people cried. So did I. I witnessed open hearts and open emotions. People were hugging each other, and it was ever so beautiful. The sad truth is that we all feel that we have more time than we actually do. So, after my request of those attending to speak freely to their significant others, I asked them all to celebrate each other and enjoy the food, drink, and dancing. And they did enjoy those things for sure. There was no wedding that night, but it was a truly beautiful party and evening.

At that point, Jamie left the stage as she had some party items to attend to. As she began to leave the room, I stopped her mid-stride. Speaking into the microphone, I told her, "Jamie, you've touched many more people than those who are here in attendance, and they wanted to give you a special gift." I had asked friends of Jamie to send in pictures of themselves and Jamie to our DJ, and he created a montage of pictures with a timeline. The pictures were shown on monitors around the room. This time, I watched the people smile and tear up with happy tears. The pictures went back to when Jamie's children were just babies, and included the friendships, the experiences, and the moments that she and her close friends and family had had together over all the years, up to that point in time. It was fabulous. Jamie was stunned. It felt heartwarming, and it made a nice segue into the rest of the evening.

The evening progressed, and it was a great, great party. The food was spectacular. Jamie and I had selected songs that had made a difference to us over the years, songs that meant something to a lot of us. The dancing and festivities progressed, and as the evening was starting to wear down, Jamie appeared from nowhere, wearing her wedding dress from our March wedding in Hawaii. I grabbed the microphone and said, "Jamie, the people here still think there should be a wedding tonight. What do I tell them or show them?"

Jamie told the DJ to play that special montage and on cue, he played our wedding video. Everyone then realized that we had gotten married on 3/23/2023! It was truly a fabulous party. What a memorable, beautiful, and loving party. Now, that's how you create a memory!

Lesson to learn:

Rely on you. This life you live day by day is not your first rodeo. You didn't get where you are by being stupid. You are smart and clever and have probably made some damn good choices along your life's path. I guess what I'm saying is for you to make your own decisions and live YOUR life for yourself. Follow that 86%-right gut of yours, and the world will be yours my friend. Like Frank Sinatra said, do it your way!

CHAPTER FIFTEEN

Love Your Own Skin

I learned something about myself. Why did I continually do things for others? Because I unconsciously wanted something from them. Why was I continually disappointed and feeling taken advantage of by people whom I was nothing but kind to? Why? It took me a lifetime to finally figure it out, but I think I've got it now.

I come from humble beginnings. We had electricity of course, a roof over our heads, and even bathrooms inside the home. We had two cars, clothes on our backs, and food, so we weren't lacking in the basics. No, we were doing fine, but not special in any way, that's for sure. I think my tendency to do things for others goes back to my younger days. Be aware that I came from the west side of Chicago—an area called Austin, near Columbus Park, where as a boy I used to walk to the park, fishing pole in hand, and spend endless hours fishing at the lagoon all by my happy self.

I've never felt inadequate or less than anyone in my life. I had a brother named "jerk-off," a true selfish prick but Jesus Christ to my parents. I knew there was something off about my brother—entitled, perhaps spoiled, but just something off about him. From my perspective, jerk-off was the favorite. This was a constant theme as I grew up. But first of all, understand something: this is not the typical sibling saying, "Mommy loved you more than me." I personally could not care one way or the other. I always thought my parents were being conned by my brother, and I just watched it over the years. As life unfolded, I actually found their interactions quite fascinating. Let me share a little of this with you. I think you'll enjoy it.

One day, it was jerk-off's turn to cut the grass. He didn't want to. Just a little whimper to Mommy and Daddy, and don't worry about it. Shelly will do it. It's Jerk off's turn to throw out the garbage, but Shelly, please do it. No problem.

I had a date for Saturday night, so I asked permission to take our "hot" Pontiac Bonneville out for that evening. Got it! So, I washed and waxed the car all day Saturday. I went inside to clean up for my date and when I came out, the car was gone because jerk-off didn't want to take his car and get it wet since it looked like a possibility of rain. He left me with the family clunker while his car, which I couldn't drive, was left sitting in the garage all prepped and proper. I had to drive the old Chrysler. I always had to take a back seat, and in this case, in the family car as well.

Other than the car incident, it really never bothered me. For some reason, after a knee-jerk response, and a roll of the eyes, I kind of enjoyed watching the family dynamics. Look at it from my perspective. (Oh, and first of all, you should know the knee-jerk reaction with the side order of eye roll was for my parents; I can't believe how my parents always caved in to that bullshit crap of my brother's.) The truth of the matter was that I found some perverse enjoyment in the solitude of whatever task I was picked or volunteered for. I could and I did, from time to time, love to cut that lawn of ours—making the rows and cutting on a diagonal. It was a form of meditation. Tranquil, in fact. So, stuff like that only reinforced my desire for the pleasure of keeping my own company in the self-imposed solitary confinement of my chores.

People wondered why I was always smiling. I think they thought I had some secret about them or life or something, and that I thought I was smarter than everybody else. They were right; that's exactly how I felt. Weird, ain't I? For some reason, it has always served me well. I guess I just like myself more than most others. And that's OK with me! Because it is true that you can't love another until you finally love yourself, and nobody loves me more than me. I'm my biggest fan, that's for sure. If not me, then, who?

This chore thing followed me. When I was in basic training in the Army, I unconsciously loved the chores. I quickly figured out that if you spoke back to your drill sergeant just a little bit, you would get punished just a little bit. Let me give you a couple of examples.

I was ordered to take a jeep over to headquarters and to be careful and safe since I was new to driving a jeep and the location was several miles away. But as military intelligence (obviously an oxymoron) decided, the papers had to be delivered to wherever "there" was. It was an opportunity for a solitary ride with the jeep, or so I thought. I don't know why I said what I did, but I blurted out to the drill sergeant, "This makes no sense to me."

He came right up to my face, since they love to do that face-to-face crap, and said, "What's the problem, maggot?"

I responded, "How could this be a safe vehicle when there aren't any seatbelts in the jeep?" and that pissed him off to no end, because I had now rejected a direct order. I looked him right in the eye and said, "Drill Sergeant, I'm sorry but I have to reject your direct order."

Now he was hot at me for embarrassing him in front of the platoon; he didn't like that—go figure!

He didn't like my response, but I could see he was the type of guy who just loved to fuck with people. And fuck with him I did, as I knew guys like him had to get the last word in, so I let him. He called me a pussy and said that those papers had to be delivered one way or the other, so he had an idea. He said with disdain that he was very sick of looking at me, but if he made me take the jeep, I would be there and back in no time and then he would have to look at me again. "But since headquarters is three-and-a-half miles away," he said, "I am really concerned about your safety." Sarcastically, he added that since it was only 95° that day and it was now only 11 a.m., it would be much safer if I double-timed all the way back to headquarters for the next couple of miles by foot. The platoon laughed, which only infuriated the drill sergeant more, so as he turned from me, he poured his wrath on them.

The drill sergeant tried to rub salt in the wound by saying, "Don't worry, maggot (they like to call you names like that), the sun will be bright and hot for the next couple of hours, so you should be safe on the trip by foot." He thought he had really punished me. *Fuck him*, I thought. All he had done was guarantee me the next two to three hours of, wait for it . . . solitude. I was alone—no, marching, no obstacle courses, no being yelled at. Nothing. Just peaceful solitude. I was happy, the drill sergeant was happy, and so was the universe. Life was good and I trotted off.

Another favorite chore of mine in the Army was K. P. Yep, "kitchen police." You've probably never heard of that, have you? Kitchen police was just that—policing the kitchen. Mopping the floor, cleaning the fryers, the grease traps, the walls, and any other shit job that helped maintain the status quo of the kitchen so they could feed thousands of soldiers a day. I forget exactly what they had me doing some days as KP, but there I was. As if he had given the instructions hundreds of times before, the jerk in charge told all of us "volunteers" to either grab a mop, a brush, a rag, or a knife and get to work. The knife sounded the easiest until I asked like a smart ass, "What is it for?"

He was obviously bothered by the burden of having to listen to my question, let alone not ready to dignify it with an answer. All of a sudden, as if on cue, this huge shape of a person came over, looked me in the eye, and said only, "Follow me."

I was taken out to a loading dock at the back of the kitchen. Before me, on the side of the dock, was a pile of potatoes about five feet tall. Hundreds and hundreds of potatoes! This pile consisted of weird-sized potatoes that could not be easily peeled by the automatic peeling machine. They still need to be peeled, but how?

The envelope, please. You got it, the knife! So, there I was, sitting my skinny ass on a bucket turned upside down. No supervisors and no time limits. Just an ever-growing pile of potatoes yelling at me to peel them. As I sat there, I felt a nice warm breeze on my face, watching the trainees marching in the sun and laughing to myself as they were yelling at me, all the while loving the solitude and peace. Even if they called it "kitchen police," life was good.

Lesson to learn:

Some people can be alone and some cannot. Don't rely on others to complete you. You are a wonderful, beautiful child of God who needs nothing more than to be. Look within yourself and revel in your own self-worth. You might like being with others as we are all social animals, but truth to tell, you must try to be happy by yourself. You cannot love another until you love yourself. Advertising tells us to be thinner, to be prettier, to be younger, but that is a fool's mission.

Do you remember my friend Bob Todd and what he said? "Be who you is."

In other words, be true to yourself. Get to know who you are and love yourself. After all, you just need to be the best version of yourself. End of lesson.

CHAPTER SIXTEEN

Just Call Me Fishface

OK, so I did my time in the army. Now what? There I was with an associate of arts degree, a Bachelor of Arts in psychology, three years of law school at night, and then a stint in the Army. What was I to do now?

Stream of consciousness, for the second or third time, means as the thoughts come to me, I can write them down regardless of the time order. So here I am, newly married for the first time, about 24 to 25 years old, and I have just accepted a job offer from my father-in-law for a whole big $300 a week! Could life get any better than this? There must be a god . . . or not. So, here's the scene. First, the perspective in my head: *Wow, an executive position for a college grad like me, learning the seafood business domestically and internationally. Buying, selling, negotiating, contracts . . . what a future!*

Now, the reality. I walked into the retail offices of my father-in-law's store (I will just call it XYZ Seafood Company. I say XYZ, because the pricks in my ex-wife's family are just that—pricks.) I'm a college grad, have been in law school, and had Army training as a combat medic. Watch out world, here I come! I got up early in the morning, showered and shaved, and I was ready.

I wore the best suit I had. I only had one to pick from so that was easy. I put on a shirt and tie, polished shoes, and looked as clean and pressed as

I could be. On to my new office.

And there I stood, dressed to the nines, standing in front of some disgusting glass displays of raw fish, both fresh and stinking. It seemed as if my future was laid out before me inside the display cases of the retail store, which was the public's view of this institution. In the showcases were assorted refrigerated products, seafood items such as cooked cocktail shrimp, herring, smoked fish of assorted species, and somebody's lunch bag that had on it, written in very bold obvious magic marker, "This ain't yours. Stay the fuck away." My future was looking bright. Or so I thought.

Behind the counter stood several low-level employees dressed in different attire, each one of them, as if in a comedy show, with the same white apron wrapped around them. I say low-level employees because I was better than all of them. You know, I came from the suburbs while they were all from the city of Chicago. I was smarter and more educated than them. However, unbeknownst to me, some of those who worked the counter were either retired or burned-out college professors and PhDs. It was just a fishbowl full of Damon Runyan characters from all of humanity. I had a lot to learn about people.

But I digress. So, there I was, nicely dressed for my first real job appearance since college and military service. I asked one of the schmucks behind the counter to tell my father-in-law that I had arrived for my first day of employment. The guy laughed at what he saw and went out towards the back. Without a telephone or intercom, he yelled out, "Mickey, there's some punk out here to see you!" The remaining people on the counter chuckled when they heard the yell, and all gathered, waiting for Mickey to appear and greet me on my first day of employment.

It took about five minutes, but out came my father-in-law and his son, the brother-in-law from hell. Before the big man could speak, the big-mouthed brother-in-law did. Obviously knowing me, he laughed and said,

"What are you dressed up for? Where are you going?"

I replied, "To WORK and I'm early." Of course, being early always makes a good impression. Like anybody could really give a shit about what I was talking about. I was the punchline of the joke for the day.

Oh yeah, they were impressed all right. My father-in-law was embarrassed for me and said to ignore his son. He told me to go outside and come around the side entrance of the store to meet him, so I did. He welcomed me and told me I didn't have to dress to impress, threw me an apron, and told me to hang my suit, tie, and coat in the closet, put on the apron, and get out on the counter.

Lesson to learn:

I'm not really sure about this chapter as I had no clue what I was getting into. Perhaps the real lesson should be: Don't let your own perceptions get fooled by somebody else's reality, especially if you have to live that reality!

CHAPTER SEVENTEEN

Welcome to 13 Years of a Shit Show

I can't believe I'm going down this rabbit hole: the memories, the stories, and it probably was the best education about life that I ever could've had. It was great. Not while I was going through it, that's for sure, but only reflecting with hindsight. If you thought I was jumping around before, then strap it on, Stewie. Back we go in the time machine to me working in the family shit show (I mean fish business). So, here's the scene: a family-owned retail store selling fish/fried shrimp/pizza/Italian beef sandwiches/hamburger/hotdog/pop out of machines/liquor/smoked fish/cocktail shrimp/smoked fish heads/whatever they could sell for a buck or two.

Yep, that's it. I wandered around that prison I had placed myself in. What did I do? The walls of the building soon turned into a prison containing my father-in-law, my brothers-in-law, and me. Talk about egos! One was ignorant, one with no people skills, and one that was just ignored. But hey, there was a paycheck, and looking at the whole scene, I quickly realized that I was a part of it. God, what did I do? Dumb ass me.

What had I done? I felt stuck in a royal family of misfits. What was my future? Selling fried shrimp to retail customers day and night? Wearing an apron to provide for my family? Future security? What the fuck!

I spent a year of delusion, a year in which I kept repeating to myself, "I have to be wrong in my perspective of this life I am in." *How could I be so wrong?* I thought, and then realized I wasn't. I wondered, *What do I do next?* I turned to one of my brothers-in-law, asking him why we didn't buy and sell in the wholesale fish market.

He yelled back, "Because we don't, that's why!" and walked off. I didn't respond; I just shook my head and thought, *What an asshole!* Two days later, he approached me in his own fucked up way and said, "The only reason we don't trade in the wholesale fish business is because we never thought about it."

He said he asked his father why they couldn't trade in the wholesale business, and he replied, "You can do that when you know the business." I always thought the father was covering up for his sons and their lack of knowing anything about the business they were in; what a circus I was working for!

About an hour later, my genius brother-in-law asked me to go outside for a cigarette and talk, and once outside, he turned to me and asked what I had in mind.

"That's the point," I said, "you've been working here for years and years, and you don't know shit about this business."

His response was like a typical 10-year-old: "Well, you don't know anything either."

Exactly my point. I said, "Send me to the Fulton Fish Market in New York City and I'll figure it out."

Again, the child responded with, "No, I want to go to New York City, not you."

"Oh," I said, "OK, you must have researched, like I did, what the Fulton Fish Market was all about, so what did you think about the facts of the place? Let me know what you think about the Fulton Fish Market having 162 wholesalers, distributors, processors, and retail outlets, what they are doing, and why you are there and not me. Good luck."

My brother-in-law came up to me later in the day and said, "How do you want the new business cards to be made out? When do you want to leave for New York?"

The conclusion, of course, was that we were then in the wholesale seafood business.

By the next week, I was in New York City. My genius brothers-in-law decided not to tell my father-in-law, who was vacationing for three months down in Florida for the winter, that I was trying to expand his business because they were afraid they would get yelled at by Daddy; it was unbelievable how these bozos thought and how they ran a business. It was absolutely astounding. Wow! In hindsight, it was probably the right call because that was around the beginning of October when the father-in-law, as I said, was out of town with his lovely wife, the mother-in-law from hell. We wouldn't see them until winter was just a faint memory. That way, no one had to listen to his bullshit, so why ask for any of it any sooner than we had to, as if the premature ejaculation of his mouth was something we desired. I don't think so!

On to my hotel in New York City, which was located somewhat near the famous Fulton Fish Market. Most people knew where the fish market was located by the smell of 162 representatives of the seafood industry. *Tomorrow is my day*, I thought. After registering at the hotel, I contacted a taxi—yes, this was before Uber—to pick me up early in the morning and take me to the fish market. I couldn't wait for dawn. It was *carpe diem*, sort of.

I waited for my cab at the appointed hour. I stood there in front of my hotel before the sun came up, and there came my cab, blinking its lights like some Soviet spy with a secret code.

I entered the taxi and we took off on our way to the bowels of the seafood industry of New York City. Fulton Fish Market, here we come! Maybe it's the romantic in me, but I cherished the very first day of my starting a new career in a new industry in a new city. Wow. The birth of a new day for so many things. I arrived at the fish market by 6 a.m.

I looked around and saw a few trucks arriving, or so I thought. Men with brushes and brooms were getting ready for a new business day. Some guys were preparing to work as they sipped their coffee in anticipation of the day. I went over to the first of 162 offices in the Fulton Fish Market and figured I would start at 7 a.m. That way I wouldn't interrupt anybody. It was 6:45 a.m., so I wandered over to the very first door on the very edge of the Fulton Fish Market. On cue at 6:46, the door I waited in front of blasted open with some guy pushing with all his might. With his right hand, he closed the door and with his left he locked it even faster and flipped a hidden sign that said "Closed – see you tomorrow."

I started to say something, and without turning around, this huge man raised his oak tree of an arm and said, "Read the sign."

I said to myself again, *WTF, where is everyone? Is this some kind of fish holiday?*

I waited and waited, but the longer I waited, the emptier the place became. I couldn't understand it. I had no chance, and I had no choice. Stupid ass me never took the cab driver's phone number so I had nothing to do but wait until 5 p.m.

When the cab driver arrived, he was laughing and asked me how I liked the market. "You were so worried about being there too early," he said, "but it turned out you were too late! They were going home when you were just getting there."

The next day at three in the morning on a cold October day, with fresh business cards in hand, there I stood. I started with the best line I could come up with, which was, "Hi, I'm Sheldon and I'm from Chicago. All I need to ask you is, what do you need and what do you have?" Most of them just looked at me, shook their heads, and kept talking on the phone, yelling at their help, or doing whatever it was they did all day long, like yelling and screaming, because nobody ever just talked in that place. With that famous line of mine, our wholesale business was born.

There I was with an associate of arts degree, a bachelor's degree, and three years of night law school before being drafted into the Army; all my education certainly did not prepare me for life in reality, where, as we say, they shoot real bullets.

Strap on buttercup; we're in for a rough ride, but I promise you it will be one of the best adventures of your life, at least vicariously; you can relive it all through me.

So, let's re-establish the environment I was in: 162 offices, 162 stairs to climb, 162 faces barking "Get the fuck out of here; we're busy!" or "I don't need anything!" I'm still not sure what he thought I was selling or why he couldn't just give me a simple "No, get out." Yep, no doubt the universe was just waiting for me to be introduced to 162 new friends I had yet to meet. After two weeks, I scheduled my flight back to Chicago with almost 100 or so business cards in hand from potential customers, and I went to work building our wholesale seafood business.

Oh, you're wondering what happened to the other 62 people I didn't get business cards from? Yes, those were the ones who told me to go fuck myself and that they were too busy. Too busy doing what? I'm still not sure.

Try to follow me, Frankie. Yes, I had done all the groundwork. Yes, I had made the effort and called on everyone, spilling my guts out, trying to find customers, and I did. But during that time, I also realized that this business was never going to be mine. This business was being run by a bunch of jackasses, and no matter what I did, it was a hell of a lot better than what they had ever done.

I also realized that I had to start my own business doing something for me, and at that time (and I know I'm jumping around again), I recalled a certain retail customer who came in, with whom I had a lot in common. His name was Norm Smith. We both worked for fathers-in-law. We were both fed up with making everyone else money, and we were both looking for something else to do in the interim. This realization came to me after I looked at the wholesale seafood business that we had started and realized I was a one-man show. It's funny that I still remember his name. Without Norm Smith, you wouldn't be reading this book. And if you look at it carefully, isn't that weird that this guy befriended me and I him? He explained a business to me and that would change everything for both him and me.

Norm and I had become friends through his frequent visits to our retail store and one day, I said to him, "Norm you look like you're doing better and better, and I'm struggling here at this company. What are you doing? Because it sounds like you're getting rid of your ex-father-in-law and moving on."

"Yes," he said, "no doubt about it. I have discovered that there is silver in X-ray film."

"What are you talking about?" I asked.

He said, "When you hold up a piece of X-ray film (remember, this is before digital), and you look at a leg bone, the white part is where the silver has washed off, but where all the black is, there is silver still present. I call on doctors and clinics for the scrap X-ray film. And the people I sell the scrap film to know how to extract the silver to make a lot of money."

Unbeknownst to me, at this time, Bunker Hunt was playing with the silver market; silver was $11 an ounce when I started into this side gig. Silver ran from $11 up to $52 an ounce, so there was certainly money to be made. . The only problem was that I didn't know how to make a dollar buying and selling X-ray film, so I said to Norm, "Hey, can we get together and talk when we're both off work?"

Norm said, "Of course. Meet me at a restaurant on Saturday morning where we can have coffee and I'll explain it to you."

Just a little reminder: Remember that I had started working for my father-in-law in a retail seafood business. I saw no future in that, so I suggested to my brother-in-law that we start a wholesale seafood business. I went to New York to talk to 162 companies and left with almost 100 business cards of people who had the potential to be either a buyer or a seller to me. But also remember, I didn't know anything about this business; I didn't know a fish from a flounder from a shrimp, but I had to learn it and learn it I did.

I also knew I had to start a separate business that no one knew about, and I guessed that silver was as good as anything else. So, to the restaurant I went on a Saturday to meet with Norm. My usual work schedule was to arrive at the retail fish store and not only the retail but the wholesale business by calling and trying to buy and sell seafood products all over the country, and then I had to run the nighttime division from 4 p.m. until 2 a.m. to continue with the retail business.

Let's just say my father-in-law was not the most compassionate of bosses. I would leave the downtown retail location a little after 2 a.m. and then take different routes home, which was an hour and a half away. The reason for the different routes was that I was taking down names of companies that either could or should have X-ray film for sale. I looked at doctors' offices and clinics as I drove, and I wrote down their names and addresses. I usually didn't get home until 4 a.m.

I decided to name my new company Mar-Cor Environmental Services, Inc., after two of my daughters, Marnie and Corie. The next day, after only four hours of sleep, the very first thing I would do was telephone the doctors and clinics whose names I had written down. Of course, it was early in the morning and nobody was at work, but I would leave my message with their answering services, briefly saying, "Please tell the person in charge that I have called. I am willing to pay cash for outdated X-ray, film."

This went on until one day, I received a telephone call at the fish store from a doctor's office that had some X-ray film for sale. This was the start of another new career. You would think that after all the jobs I decided to work at, I should have been rolling in money, but the truth of the matter is that my father-in-law paid me a whole big $300 a week for indentured servitude.

My idea was that Mar-Cor Environmental Services could be a premier silver recovery business. I could run it as a professional operation with suits and ties, as the only competition I had were people like Norm, who went around with a pocket full of cash and blue jeans and tried to talk to the help in the back room and pay them off so they could buy or steal (or both) the X-ray film. So, I looked at my current situation after several months and did an assessment.

The situation at Mar-Cor Environmental Services was that we had telephone operators, cold callers, salespeople, secretaries, installers of silver, recovery equipment, truck drivers, and freight people for those long hauls when we needed a truck to pick up large volumes of X-ray film. Yep, all these people were rolled up into one. You got it. I was a one-man band. I think it was when I was trying to type an invoice, (yes, typing—we did not have computers then), and suffering from a bad cold that I had an epiphany. I think I had a sneezing jag, during which I violently sneezed and pressed my face into the keyboard of the typewriter and cut the bridge of my nose. And I started to laugh at myself.

Call it an epiphany, or maybe it was just a realization that I had to hire people. I couldn't do it by myself anymore. I was actually building a business and having a blast doing it. Rather than take you through the daily put-out-the-fire scenarios, I think you will enjoy this more if we talk about the lessons learned and how if you listen to the signs, you won't have to go through the grief I did from the lessons I learned. So, I guess I'll pick and choose the lessons that make the most sense to me, or at least those that didn't destroy me.

Lesson to learn:

There is no lesson for this chapter. Why, you might ask? Because I didn't know enough to even formulate a question. I learned as I went and as I made each move. One move led me in another direction, to another crossroad and another path less traveled. I didn't know what the hell I was doing other than to keep on doing it, and that I guess that's the lesson.

Once you start going, keep going. Once you start doing, keep doing. Eventually, when you're tired enough or exhausted from your task, you'll look up and see where you are and what you've accomplished. It's hard to put into words the lesson to be learned, but if anything, it's that persistence and determination will take you farther than a good education or brilliance. I know it sounds too simplistic, but that's all I have.

CHAPTER EIGHTEEN

Respect

I think the best general rule that has far-reaching effects on so many is the simple concept of respect. It didn't matter who I came across; the common thread for all was that at the end of the day, we all just wanted to get home, have peace, and be loved by our families, and if not by the family then perhaps by the family dog or cat or goldfish. You see, we all want to be complete and happy and safe. So, since we all want similar things, we already have things in common. And it just comes down to respect. Common, everyday respect. This is the commonality that we are all enjoying. Respect—such a simple concept. We can't literally walk in someone else's shoes, but it doesn't matter. What matters is having empathy, common compassion, and a love for your fellow man.

Here's another, more obvious example: In order for me to grow my business, I had to call on owners of companies. What could I possibly have in common with these company owners? I started almost every introduction of myself to my prospective new account with, "You and I have a lot in common."

"What's that?" they asked.

"We can both contribute a chapter or two to the book of ex-employees!"

With that, they would usually laugh and say, "Isn't that the truth! And now, with commonality, we were friends, even buddies if you will.

And another account was in the books. Good job.

Remember that as I was building my business, I was still working at the fish company. My routine was as follows: I had to be at the fish company at 4 p.m. Why? Because I had to run the retail operation from 4 p.m. until 2 a.m. This meant feeding the retail customers, making pizzas, delivering food orders, and whatever it took. I guess I was a renaissance man; if we were short on delivery drivers, I was in my car delivering. If the grease in the fryers needed changing, I changed it. Or I did whatever else, whatever shit job there was because my father-in-law loved to punish people with bullshit.

I should clarify something for you. While I was building the fish business, I was also building my business. Yeah, I worked nights, holidays, and weekends. That was my punishment for trying to do my own thing. He thought he could wear me out and that I would give up, but he didn't know me at all. Did I start my business before I was truly ready? Probably. But youth and eagerness are pretty much connected.

I could make a whole book out of this part of the story but let me just make a long story short. I quit my job in the fish business. I thought I was ready, but I fell flat on my ass. I'm jumping around, and I'm sorry, but soon you will understand. Let's wrap up this chapter on respect before I clarify for you what was going on.

So, there I was, working two jobs, living on four to five hours of sleep, and working myself like a rented mule. I remember as if it were yesterday turning to a coworker out of frustration and asking him that question. You know, sometimes there are names and events that happen in our lives that seem like yesterday, and other times you just can't remember shit.

His name was Bob Todd. He was a Black gentleman, extremely well educated, which was obvious when he spoke. Bob was one of those wandering souls that the world just wasn't ready for. He was a very interesting man, almost intoxicating—a great storyteller, a realist, and he also had a very funny perspective on life. I remember that once we were talking about money, and Bob said, as usual in a sarcastic manner, that there were only three ways to get rich. The first was to win the lottery. The second was to inherit wealth from a rich relative, and the third way, at least in his perspective, was to fuck somebody out of it! Perhaps it was a bit bitter, but funny nevertheless.

I turned to Bob one evening while working the counter when business was slow, and he caught a glint in my eye. "What's the matter buddy?" he asked. "What's bothering you; what's on your mind?"

I took a breath and let out a big sigh. I said, "Bob I am busting my ass working two jobs. I sleep four to five hours a night, I'm working seven days a week with family obligations and expenses, and I don't know who I am anymore or what I should be doing."

He looked at me for a moment and said, "Shelly, I like you. You're funny, smart, and have a great work ethic. You just can't see in yourself what I see in you, so listen. I'm quitting tomorrow, so you won't see me again. It's time for me to move on just like you."

"What do you mean, Bob?"

He said, "Just remember this Shelly: Be who you is and not who you ain't, 'cause if you is who you ain't, you ain't who you is."

We both laughed at his words, but I thought about it long and hard. You've got to be honest with yourself. You've got to see your perspective in a reality that is harsh and raw perhaps, but true nevertheless. Life is not the way we want it to be. It is the way it is and these rules of law, these messages, these little sayings hit home to me hard, very hard.

He was such an eloquent man, and so on the spot. "Remember these words and good luck," he said to me. "By the way, do you mind if I leave early? I have packing to do."

I said, "Of course." He handed me his apron and I never saw him again, but I got the message: I had to be true to myself, and I have been ever since..

I had to be focused and focus I did. I was laser-focused. I knew what I had to do and the only adjustment I had to make was getting more sleep (lol). Mar-Cor Environmental Services, here we come.

I could go on and on about building my company for almost 45 years, and the lessons learned while doing it. Some lessons we repeat as if we didn't learn them right the first time, and then we shall certainly repeat them over again. I will share other examples of these everyday lessons, but for now, I must leave you with one thought. My father-in-law had a cousin named Lester. He was a professional chef at the Continental Hotel in downtown Chicago. You probably don't know about this hotel, but it was the place to be, and he was the man in charge of the entire operation as far as food goes. The Continental Hotel went the same way as Enron and Pan Am Airlines. They went out of business, but my father-in-law found a bit of empathy and gave Lester a job as a cook in the retail joint. I know people, and I can tell a lot just by talking with someone for a few minutes. And I could tell that Lester was one of those guys.

Lester knew what he had to do. He couldn't stand the way he was treated, let alone working in a fish joint after being a big shot at the Continental Hotel. My father-in-law had a way of finding someone's weakness and then exploiting it to his benefit. He was a prick, no doubt about it. I don't know what he paid Lester but I'm sure it was nowhere near what he was used to earning. I could see it on his face—he was in financial trouble. But even though he had his own difficulties, he would always take the time to say to me, "Hey kid, how's that business of yours doing? How many accounts do you have?"

And I remember like it was yesterday, telling him, "I've got 18 now and it's really growing. I think I've got something here."

"Good for you," he would always reply. "This place is not for you; start your own business and do your own thing. Mickey (my father-in-law) only cares about Mickey, so fuck him."

I remember having to have a talk with my father-in-law about my being late to the retail counter as I was starting to get busy with the silver business. My arrival time of 4 p.m. stretched to 4:15 to 4:30 and then to 5 p.m. and even later because I was at appointments or doing installations or selling on the phone. I was a busy guy. But my father-in-law was not concerned about my business; he was concerned about his counter, his money, his income, not mine.

My usual day went like this: up by 6 a.m., personal grooming, and then on the phones by eight. Or I was in the car to go install silver recovery equipment, or putting on a suit for a sales presentation. Every day was different, and I wore all the hats—a real one-man show. And, of course, I had to be at the counter at 4 p.m. until 2 a.m., after which I would drive home an hour or more taking down names of prospective clients. What a life! It was lots of work, but I loved every minute of it.

Lesson to learn:

Not a big lesson. Just respect humanity and stay focused on your goal no matter how your distracted life might try to get you off course. Don't let someone else pull your strings. Do what you must to get through the day or the task. Whatever the moment brings you, always, in the back of your mind, keep focused on yourself and your goals before anyone else's.

CHAPTER NINETEEN

Sorry You See It That Way

In hindsight, my father-in-law was not wrong. I had a job; I was supposed to be working at 4 p.m. at the counter and that's that. I get it. I got it, but I didn't see it that way. Remember, I had been trying to improve myself in every way possible, and that included reading self-help books. I read everything I could get my hands on. Now it was time to implement what I had been reading.

I had graduated from college. Yay! However, that doesn't really provide a person with the practical education they need for life. As I said, I had read every self-help book I could get my hands on. Here are the ones I picked to start my education:

Think and Grow Rich by Napoleon Hill.

Winning Through Intimidation by Robert Ringer

Pulling Your Own Strings by Wayne Dyer

Gorilla Marketing (by some gorilla)

Great books, great foundation for anybody who wants to expand and show the world who they are. These are the books that will give you a good start. One day, my father-in-law said to me, "Hey, forget about that side business you have with the silver stuff; the money is on the counter here in the store and not with X-ray film."

I just looked at him and said, "I'm sorry you see it that way."

"What way?" he asked.

"Your way, not my way," I said.

With that, he replied, "You'd better come in at 2 p.m., not 4 p.m., starting tomorrow."

I just looked at him, took off my apron, and said, "I quit!" Out the door I walked, heart in my throat but nevertheless okay. I had a new career ahead. I was only working half days, but that soon became 12 hours a day. I worked day and night hauling X-ray films in my car, typing invoices, arriving in my suit for sales presentations. I worked like a dog until after three months of exhaustion, I finally herniated a disc and ended up in the hospital for a couple of weeks. It was time to regroup. I needed to hire people, but how could I afford that?

A friend of mine told me, "You can't afford to NOT hire someone." And so, the building of the business started in earnest. I'm not going to bore you with the day-to-day tasks, just the lessons learned along the way. I learned many lessons along the 45-year journey of building my business. Some of the lessons learned have been painful. Trusted people, family members, relatives—we all have stories. So, here's a lesson I learned early on:

Remember, I was working at the fish store at night and doing my business in the day from 8 a.m. until I had to be downtown at the fish joint at 4 p.m. And remember that I ended up in the hospital due to exhaustion and a herniated disc. Once I was released from the hospital, I still needed to rehabilitate. It was freezing in Chicago, and I couldn't take a chance of slipping on the ice and ending up back in the hospital. My mother-in-law offered me their Florida condo in which to rest and recuperate. My father-in-law said I could have two weeks there, but that was my winter vacation and then I would have to return to work. What a prick he was! My business only earned money when I was gathering X-ray film and reselling it.

I came up with the idea of a postcard campaign inspired by the book

Gorilla Marketing, and bought a list of doctors' and X-ray clinics in Florida. I also offered cash for X-rays and mailed out hundreds of postcards before I left for Florida. I did not get a great response from the mailing, but all I needed was a few replies.

Sure enough, I received a call from a young girl who said her father was a doctor in Florida and he had passed away, leaving a lifetime's worth of X-rays in his garage. I drove over to her dad's home and was floored to see more X-rays than I had ever seen from one doctor. I was so excited! As I recall, I had a total of $9000 in cash. The price I had quoted her had to include the cost of freight home, so we weighed up all the material, multiplied it by the price I was willing to pay per pound, and agreed on the sale.

Not so fast, Frankie! Yes, we agreed on the sale, but I only had half the amount of cash I owed her, as I had never expected to get that much material from one location, let alone the entire mailing. She got nervous and didn't want to take a chance on me paying her once I got the film delivered. How could I guarantee the payment to her? I was desperate for that film and the profit that I was going to make in order to pay bills at home. Quickly I came up with a plan. "Here is $9000," I said, "and I will only take the film that $9000 will cover. Give me your word that you will hold the rest for me, and I'll send you the balance by check. Once you cash the check, let me know when I can arrange to pick up the load. She agreed and we shook hands. We both kept our word; I sent the check, she shipped the film, and we were both happy.

Lesson to learn:

Again, sometimes you just have to read people and go with your gut. I did, she did, and we were both happy. Just as a sidenote (and I know I am repeating mentioning that article I read, but it bears repeating, so listen and read it):

I recently read an article about a study done at Harvard, concerning what we sometimes refer to as our gut feeling. Sometimes, for no reason whatsoever, we get a feeling in our gut that this or that is not right, or maybe it is. It's just an impulse, but the study proved that 86% of the time we trust our gut, it's right. So, if you go with your gut feeling, as the expression says, it is 86% more likely that things will work out for you.

CHAPTER TWENTY

And Sometimes the Gut Ain't Enough

So, Frankie, fast-forward to my early days as a refiner/smelter. Hot stuff! (Industry joke.) I'm not going to bore you with the industry terms, so let's just say I figured out a way for jewelers, pawn shops, and printers nationwide to increase the revenue on the scrap they refined every month or every quarter. If they sent their materials to me, I would show them the increased value and the system I came up with.

Over the years, from time to time, friends, family, and others would stop into the refinery with such a small amount of material that I could not do a separate refining lot for them, but I never wanted to hurt their feelings so I would usually pay them anywhere from $20 to $50 out of my pocket. Away they would go, and I just put their scrap in a drawer and forgot about it: an earring, a ring that was unloved, a charm bracelet, and other things like that. Nothing big. Remember, I was always sensitive to people's feelings, and I never wanted to insult anybody.

I had probably been doing that for about 10 years when one day while doing some cleaning up, I looked into the drawer I had ignored for quite some time. I realized I had quite a bit of scrap gold in there.

It was fashionable in those days for people to pay huge money for gold chain bracelets. Why should I lay out money for something I already had? I just needed the scrap gold and someone in the business of casting gold.

Remember, I was refining precious metals, not producing jewelry. I am not a fabricator of precious metals.

I asked around the refining community for a recommendation of who might cast some gold for me. I had a very good reputation in the film-washing business and silver recovery as well, but I did not know anybody in the gold-casting business. One name kept repeating as a reference. It was George. He was the casting man to go to for anything gold. George was located in downtown Chicago, a pain in the ass to get to but his reputation preceded him. He had instructed me to bring down my scrap gold, and he would meet me at his office, give me a tour of his factory, and I could watch my gold being melted.

George was a decent guy. I had a good vibe from him as I introduced myself to him at his location in Chicago. Of course, in those days you had to go meet somebody in person because there were no websites to look at, nor did Zoom exist, because there was no Internet.

Also, there were no computers! So, here's how his process worked. I dropped off the scrap on Monday. I told him I had melted enough metal in my day, so I didn't need to watch my metal melt. I trusted him. He said he would melt my material on Tuesday, finish the manufacturing process by Wednesday, and I could pick it up by Friday, just to be safe. "Perfect," I said, thinking this should work out really well. And that's how it went . . . well, almost.

I dropped the gold off, no problem. George melted the gold, no problem, George poured, polished, and finished the gold casting, no problem. I received the call to pick up the goods Friday morning. Great, I was on a roll . . . until there was a problem, a big one—about $1250 of a problem.

You see, George was a man of integrity. He knew that when you press or cast gold through a mold, there is always a residue of gold remaining from the pour and casting, often referred to as a "button." So, now you know that there is a button of gold after a mold is poured, and *I* know there's a button left after a casting pour (at least now, as I was warned to always ask for the button if you have something cast). And guess who else knew that fact? Yep, George knew that as well, and that's why when I called George to inquire about my button, he acknowledged it immediately when he said, "Oh shit, I never gave you the button from the pour. Sorry, but I have to reheat the furnace to extract it. I have two customers waiting for me, and we're closing soon because it's 2 p.m. on a Friday."

Great, I was 50 miles from downtown Chicago on a Friday afternoon, and the last thing I wanted to do was drive into the city, especially with the parade that was scheduled for that day. It wasn't going to happen. As I said, George was a decent guy. He was a standup guy, and he knew I was upset. He could tell from my tone on the telephone (we didn't have cell phones then) that I wasn't happy, but he tried to reassure me and calm me down. George tried to comfort me by expressing his sincerity and by assuring me the gold button would be waiting for me whenever I could come back.

"Come Monday afternoon," he said. "Show up whenever. Whatever you want; don't worry about it. I feel so bad about forgetting something so elementary, so you know what? There will be no charge for the casting. It was your gold, you were patient, I screwed up, and I know we're going to do a lot of business together in the future. I can tell, so this one's on me; just come in and get your gold button."

I thought to myself, *Wow, what a standup guy he is!* "OK," I said, "I will stop in on Monday, and I really appreciate your sincerity. I mean, it's still gold, it's still money, and it's significant enough that I have to have it."

"Of course," he said, "I totally understand." And then he said those magic words, "It's not like I'm going to die over the weekend!"

Motherfucker! Had to say it, didn't he? Couldn't just say, "See you on

Monday," . . . nope!

There I was on Monday morning, waiting in front of George's door, watching for the Store lights to come on at 8 a.m., 9 a.m., and 10 a.m. I rang the bell and slapped on the door because everyone else on the floor was open. After my banging on the door for a bit, the guy at the neighboring company opened his door and came over to see what the commotion was. I gave him the George story, and he said, "Oh, didn't you hear? He died over the weekend. His wife is handling everything. She'll take care of you."

Oh, yeah! I called her and told her what I was there for. She checked and said, "Nope, nothing here. I've got a customer to take care of." And click, the line went dead. Although I lost my $1250, I did feel as if I helped the family out with some funeral expenses since they stole my gold, the fucking thieves. It was another variation of "isn't that weird!" Life is weird, and in so many and glorious ways. But upon closing this chapter, I reflect and realize that however my life has gone, the direction has always been improving, and I'm having a blast doing it.

Life is good.

Lesson to learn:

When you need to get something done, do it now. Don't put anything off because the only thing constant in life is change and believe me, things can change fast.

AT LEAST IT DID FOR GEORGE

CHAPTER TWENTY-ONE

Anyone Got a GPS?

So where do we go from here? And what direction do we go? And what lesson do we learn? There's no right, no wrong, no up, no down; we can't be in or out so now we must become philosophical and look for the forest and not the trees, or both. Shades of Forrest Gump.

There's really no good or bad, if you think about it. Of course, there is if you press me. But what I mean is that life seems to be constantly moving little by little, perhaps just by degrees in one direction or another, or both. It is a life of millimeters. Are you happy? Yeah, kind of, but with a little sadness around the corner, and then blue skies until....

"Until" is another definition word, but as we age, we just notice these things more—the terms, and of course the meanings. Earlier, I spoke about perspectives, and I think the more we age, the more we have to be aware of our perspectives because the real truth is that if you're not happy with where you're at, change your perspective and you will change your reality. Of that, I am positive.

Perhaps it's that many of the words we use are definition words. It all depends on who is using them and in what context they are spoken. It's kind of like the big difference between someone six years old and someone 60 years old. Yes, they are both aging but it certainly doesn't mean the same to both of them, does it? I'm starting to wander with my thoughts, so I'm going to take a break and I'll be back.

OK, so I am back and reflecting on what I just said about definition words. Let me give you some examples. Take the word "sale." We see it in neon everywhere we go. There are probably many types of sales: the fire sale, the going out of business sale, the discount sale, and of course, the super sale. Don't forget the other distinctive definitions of the word. All these examples are twofold. One is what the word means to those who are selling, and the other is what the word means to those who are buying. Two totally different interpretations. Are you getting the drift, Donald?

Words, terms, definitions—all have different meanings to all the different people reading something, and to those who are writing it. Be careful out there. People are deceptive everywhere, so just be aware. I'm sure there are lots of honest people (whatever the word "honest" means) and I'm sure there are plenty of deceitful people out there, (whatever the word "deceitful" means). It's what I think is honest versus what you think is honest, and everybody justifies their own interpretation. I think the next chapter will make you aware of how people justify what they do.

Lesson to learn:

Caveat emptor, let the buyer beware. They shoot real bullets in reality land.

CHAPTER TWENTY-TWO

Glazing Fish

I think you'll enjoy this story. It's really kind of funny and through it, I can show you what greed will do to a situation. I was rocking in the fish business, trying to learn everything and trying to figure out the angles and the shortcuts that could make a lot more money than the usual $.03-$.04 per pound of fish products that the industry was used to working on. I remember I was down in Miami calling on some local seafood distributors. It was a hot sunny day, but when I approached the front desk asking for the man in charge at one particular fish distributor, I was told he was in the back glazing fish. I didn't know what the hell they were talking about, but to the back I went.

When I approached the people in the backyard of the plant, the sight that met me was almost comical. Several men were taking huge pieces of frozen cod out of soggy boxes, along with other assorted seafood items apparently in the process of thawing out. I asked one of the workers what was going on, and he said the main freezer had gone on the fritz and they were trying to save the frozen products. I still didn't understand what they were doing, but they took all the nearly thawed seafood products and sprayed them with cold water before putting them into boxes to re-freeze. They would continue doing this until they had built up a sufficient glaze of ice on the product in order to save it from being freezer-burned and ruined. As I watched, I spoke with the owner about buying and selling while an idea brewed in my brain.

When I returned from Miami, I asked for a meeting with the clowns who ran the company I worked for. I explained to them that we could re-glaze all the fish products we were offering to the public, as well as to wholesale markets, and increase profits by selling these products with increased ice on them. In other words, we would be making dollars per pound for selling water. They looked at me like I had two heads but knew there was money to be made by defrauding the public and wholesale customers. I'm not proud of the fact that I was thinking devious thoughts. Actually, let's get right to the point of the matter. I was suggesting that we should cheat customers. In hindsight, of course, it was the wrong thing to do. I thought they would just put a little ice on the materials, and we would make a few ounces of a pound per piece on every pound we sold. But not these clowns! Nope, they agreed and they saw big $. Let me explain. Let's talk about shrimp.

Shrimp are graded by how many there are to a pound, so let's start with a really large shrimp: 10 to 15 pieces per pound of individually quick-frozen shrimp, called IQFs. From there they drop to 15/20's, 21/25's, 26/30's, 31/35's, and down from there. Remember these are the number of shrimp that make up one pound. The bigger the number, the smaller the size of shrimp in a pound.

The price of shrimp is, of course, directly related to the size of the shrimp. We're going to make up numbers just for discussion, so let's say that 10/15's sell for $5.00 per pound. 15/20's sell for $4.75 per pound, and 21/25's sell for $4.50 per pound. So, pay attention here, Peter; 26/30's sell for $3.75 per pound as they start to appear small in size. This was the size where I saw opportunity and heard that opportunity shouting at me to notice it.

The difference in cost between the largest shrimp as they get smaller is roughly .25 per pound. But notice the price drop from 21/25's to 26/30's. It's .75 per pound. And in the fish business, that's a lot of money. So, the play was to take 26/30 shrimp, run them through our glazing machine, which was my brother-in-law's idea since he was an engineer and could make the 26/30's larger by adding ice to them, and then they would become a 21/25. We would make up the difference between the two sizes, or the "spread," as we called it.

The idea was good. We hatched the plan and the machine did the work. And if the engineer brother-in-law is reading this, you did a damn good job, buddy. We took 26/30 shrimp from Vietnam, which are excellent shrimp by the way, marked them as a product of Mexico, and sold them as the larger size. Deceitful . . . absolutely, but more like stealing if you wish to call it what it truly was. Back in those days, we just didn't think about the consequences of our actions.

We were selling these three-pound bags of shrimp to wholesalers, who then sold them to restaurants. This was a very profitable business for quite a while. Not only were we making extra money by glazing the product, but we were also misrepresenting the source of the product as the Gulf of Mexico instead of Vietnam. It was raining money.

And here is where greed raised its ugly head. You see, we were also selling seafood to the general public, calling it "wholesale prices direct to the public." We took boxes of assorted seafood after it was glazed, repackaged them, and placed them in boxes on the floors or in freezer cases.

Let me say, at this part of the story, that I was wrong, naïve, and stupid. I thought no one would notice, until one day, after a weekend sale at which we sold this wholesale seafood to the public, a disgruntled customer came in with a bag that was 50% water and 50% shrimp. Unbeknownst to me, my greedy ex-father-in-law decided to adjust the glazing machine and slowed it down so that instead of it putting a few ounces of ice on the entire three pounds of shrimp, for every three pounds of shrimp we sold, almost a pound of it was water. It didn't take long for the city's weights and measures department to pay us a visit, and of course, the greedy father-in-law was cited and had to pay a substantial fine.

Not only had we been glazing shrimp, but my father-in-law had instructed the people at night to continue to glaze every item we sold, including fish fillets and lobster tails. At that time, lobster tail was going for almost $10 a pound, so if we added a quarter pound or half a pound of ice, that was a lot of money. I looked at my father-in-law and said, "What were you thinking?" I was as guilty as him, and I knew that this company was not my future.

To be honest, I should have been embarrassed, but I was only ticked off because I got caught and became the fall guy for his greed and my idea of glazing . . . which, I guess was correct, to be honest.

Lesson to learn:

Wrong is wrong.

You can't justify it; you can't blame someone else. You have to put on your big-boy pants and recognize that you were wrong. You deceived people and you cheated—everything the Ten Commandments tell you not to do, so whatever result you get from your actions, you probably deserve it. Honesty, fraud, cheating— they are all definition words, but you really know when the truth hits you in the face, as we must be accountable for our actions. I could go on and on with stories of the seafood business, but it was a real school in which I learned not only that business but how to do business and how not to do business. Let's just say it

---

was time to get out and it was a lot easier to sleep at night when not worrying about what official was going to come in the next day and fine us for this or that. It just wasn't a way to live.

And here I am, feeling all the guilt, and I didn't even own any part of the business. I was just an employee, but I treated it like it was my own. I was embarrassed about my actions, and I knew my time was short.

CHAPTER TWENTY-THREE

*If You Didn't Learn from the Above Lesson Maybe
This One Will Wake You, Wally*

One more visit to the seafood business. Buckle up, buttercup; this one will shake you to your core. As you know, I started the wholesale seafood business by going to New York City and learning the business firsthand from the rough guys in the Fulton Fish Market. I talked, I bullshitted, I lied. I made up whatever stuff possible to get the customers I needed in order to build a business. Most of the time, I called on strangers. I did what old-time salesmen call "cold calling." You know—you get on the phone and call someone you don't know, trying to build a relationship and see what you can do for them. You either buy or sell products they might sell or need.

Today, salespeople don't employ that type of marketing. That's what I was raised on. That's what I did, and I did it well. I was able to establish relationships by speaking to people. One of those people, I will just call Customer X, because I don't want his name out there, and you'll understand why when you read what happened.

Business was good. I bought and sold seafood from people all over the United States. Because of my schooling, and being that the seafood business came originally and mostly from New York City, it was one of my favorite places to contact new customers.

Remember, I told you my father-in-law was a tough old guy. In fact, they called him a "Westside cowboy." That part of the city, in the old days, was where the rough and tumble guys came from, and he was definitely one of them. Yes, I said the tough guys, and I'm not just talking bruisers. I'm talking mafia people. Yes, they really exist. And yes, my father-in-law knew them. He grew up with them. I had had enough of my father-in-law—the deception, the stealing, the glazing, the selling water—and thinking about all the tricks of the industry, I knew I had had enough.

We were a very successful business. We had a wholesale division. We had a retail division of three stores. We had a Chinese restaurant division that consisted of well over several hundred customers. The money was coming in hand over fist, and all as a result of ideas that I had come up with in my effort to establish a seafood dynamo from what was previously just a small seafood store in Chicago. Yes, I'm taking the credit for it, because I did the work. It was something else! But remember, I owned nothing. I was just a son-in-law working in a company for some clowns who didn't even understand what the hell they had. I had a father-in-law and two brothers-in-law who were a joke.

My father-in-law really wasn't that bad of a guy. He was just rough, and that's OK. I learned a lot from him. I guess deep down, I loved the guy, and I felt we both had a mutual respect for each other, and an ability to make things happen. But the two brothers-in-law were jokes. One was a big mouth who knew nothing about anything, other than yelling and screaming. And the other one was a smart guy who had no business being there, as he was an electronic engineer (or as they call them, a double E), but he couldn't make a living in spite of himself. He just didn't know how to get out of his own way. I don't really want to talk about family relationships, because they played out as I knew they would. The big mouth went to work at the exchange because in my opinion, he couldn't take the crap from his father anymore. He made a fairly good living, or at least he talked that game. The other one ended up back in the computer business, which he knew well, and it appeared that was really his love. Selling fish, not so much.

But I'm getting ahead of myself. The business was booming, and money rolled in, bringing more cash than you could even imagine. The way the family was set up, or at least the way I was told it was, you had to have another kid in order to get a raise. Crazy, huh? I went to my father-in-law, as my wife was pregnant, and said, "Hey, we are having a baby I need a raise, so do I get my $25 raise now?"

He looked at me with a smirk on his face. He said, "What are you talking about? I've decided we're going to play another game."

I said, "What are YOU talking about?"

"We're going bankrupt," he replied. "I figured out a way to make a profit by fucking people." .

I looked at him and said, "Are you out of your mind? There isn't enough money coming in *now* for you?"

Interest rates were sky high; the economy was in trouble; people and businesses couldn't pay their bills with 17% interest rates from the banks, and most businesses weren't doing great, although ours was . . . or so I thought. During the last several weeks, I had been getting more and more calls about the wholesale bills not being paid and whenever I asked, I was told the same thing: "Don't worry about it; the check's in the mail." How could we do so much business and yet our wholesale bills were not getting paid on time? Unbeknownst to me, the big boss had been skimming cash like a drunken sailor from retail stores in order to fund his future bankruptcy scheme. I thought, *When do I awake from this nightmare?*

He said to me, "I can tell from your performance lately that you don't want to bust your ass the way you did before, all because I won't pay you any more money."

I looked at him and said, "Are you crazy? I've made you so much money you don't even know where to put it all. He just looked at me and told me to start buying for the wholesale department because Christmas was right around the corner. I believe it was September or October. Understand that we had large freezers in the downtown location. I mean big-ass freezers that could hold a truckload of material if necessary.

He said if I wanted to keep my job, he would tell me what he wanted me to do and I would follow his orders or I could get the hell out. I was a little freaked out by his comments. I had two and a half kids to take care of, along with a wife and a home, let alone constant bills because my wife seemed to have a problem with shopping.

"All right," I said, "what do you want me to do?" I knew I had no choice but to listen to him if I wanted to have at least some money coming in. He told me he wanted me to start buying lobsters, shrimp, and every type of seafood I could get my hands on. I replied to him that we were barely able to pay our bills, saying, "You realize that these are not gentle folk we are dealing with, and if we don't pay them on time, there's gonna be hell to pay."

Without an ounce of guilt and knowing what he planned to do, he just said, "Start and when we can't put more into the freezer, that's when you're gonna stop. Don't worry; the bills will get paid."

I didn't like the idea of intentionally trying to screw people over, but I had no choice. I felt like a Nazi soldier just following orders but knowing there was going to be a nightmare—that a holocaust was coming.

At that point, I refused to sell any more seafood over the phone. My father-in-law was pissed at me, but I said I didn't care. "I'm done doing wholesale work for you on the phone if you're gonna screw everybody over eventually."

He told me to go to the retail store and start working the counter if I didn't want to get on the phone.

I had no problem doing that because at least I had an income. Perhaps two weeks went by, maybe three, and while I was at the retail counter, an average-looking guy came in and asked for Shelly. I said, "Yes, that's me."

He said, "Oh, I'm so and so from New York City. We have a mutual friend, and I told him I'd stop by and say hello for him.

"Who is that?" I asked.

"Mr. Ralph."

Hearing that name made me gulp very hard. I knew that we owed him at least $30,000 and it had been well over 30 days.

"The guy said I should come by and ask for you," said the visitor. (His name wasn't really Ralph, but for this book, Ralph will do.) "He also mentioned to me that you owe him some money. You know he's a really good guy, and he says you are too, so why don't you send him the money? You don't wanna aggravate this guy." And with that, he turned around and walked out.

Once he was out the door, I felt a panic in my body. This Mr. Ralph was no lightweight. In fact, I remember calling on him in New York, and he gave me an opportunity; for that, I was grateful. However, I knew he also kept a pair of brass knuckles on his desk as a paperweight—a sign that he was not a person to mess with.

I immediately went to my father-in-law and told him what had happened and that I had a bad feeling about it. "You'd better send the guy a check," I said.

"OK, OK, I'll take care of it. Don't worry about it," was his only response. Almost two weeks to the day, guess who came back into the store? Yes, you got it. The same guy who came just to say hello.

He said he was staying in Chicago for quite a while, and Mr. Ralph said he still hadn't gotten his check. "I really think it's in your best interest to pay him. Might not be good for your health if you don't." He turned around and left.

I felt my gut tighten and I knew this was not going to be good. I immediately went back to my father-in-law and told him what had happened. "Oh, don't worry," he said. I'll get that check out this week."

That gave me some relief until about one week later when our friend showed up one more time. It was kind of cold out in Chicago in those days, and the guy who was visiting from New York came in wearing a nice leather jacket. It was buttoned up. He said, "I had a nice long talk with Mr. Ralph last night on the phone, and he said I should come by once more, so here I am."

This time he unbuttoned the front of his jacket so that only I could see what was under it. There it was— a 45-caliber gun stuffed in the front of his pants. He made sure I got a full view of it. With that, he said, "Like I said, this is not going to be good for your health. You'd better pay him. I'll be back."

I went to my father-in-law and said, "I'm not gonna get killed by this guy. Pay the man."

He said, "OK, OK. Come on. I'll take you back to the safe." Once we got to the safe, I felt he was going to just get the money and pay the man when he came in the next time. Nope, that wasn't the case. You know what he did? He reached into the safe, brought out a 38-caliber, and said, "Here, carry this just in case he comes back."

I looked at him and said, "Are you out of your fucking mind? I'm gonna get in a gunfight with someone over money *you* owe? That's not gonna happen!" And I walked out to my car and left early for the day.

One week later, guess who came to visit again, only this time he wasn't looking friendly. He called me over and before he could get any words out,

I said, "Look," pointing to my father-in-law. "I just work here. I don't control who gets paid or what; *that* man does. His name is Mickey, and if you want your money, he's the man you need to talk to." With that, I called over to Mickey and said, "Here, you guys need to have a talk. I'm out of here."

They had a little discussion that didn't take more than five minutes and the next thing I knew, Mickey and my frequent flyer visitor went back to the office, and I heard the safe being opened. As the man left, he looked at me and said, "Smart move, kid."

Lesson to learn:

Oh, I learned all right. I learned there are things you can do, things you should do, and things you should never do. And one of those things you never do is mess with these kinds of people. Everything in life seems to be a game. You've got to know the rules. You've got to know when you can only go so far and not cross that line. The ex- father-in-law didn't care about the rules. He thought he could play by his own rules, and guess what? It never helps. It never works. It never ends pretty. I felt like I had nearly missed a bullet, and I think I really did.

CHAPTER TWENTY-FOUR

Fast-Forward 45 Years

Looking back at what I have been through in the past 45 years can only be explained with a little joke. So, bear with me Bruce; it's a short joke. A snail was crawling down the road, going as fast as a snail could go, when all of a sudden, a turtle jumped out of the bushes as fast as a turtle can jump out of the bushes. The turtle beat up the snail. He stole all the snail's money and ran, or rather crawled, off. A week later, the snail arrived at the police station to report the theft and assault. Why did it take a week for him to report what happened to him? Pay attention out there. This is a snail we're talking about. They don't go so fast. It takes them a while to get around. When the snail went to the police to report the incident, the detective at the station asked him if he could answer just one question. The snail said, "Ask me." The detective said, "Do you think you can identify the turtle that did this to you?" The snail hesitated for a moment and then said "No, I don't think I could." The detective asked him, "Why not?" And the snail replied, "It all happened so fast!"

PERSPECTIVES, IT'S ALWAYS
ABOUT THE PERSPECTIVES

Let's talk a bit about perspectives again. Let's say I lay a pen down in front of three people and ask them to describe the pen to me. One might describe its color: it's a dark blue or it's black or whatever other color it might appear to him. The next fellow might say it's a very sleek, long, slender ink pen that looks like it would be very comfortable to hold. And the last person might say it looks like a cheap way to communicate with somebody who comes from the old days. We all describe things differently or perceive things according to our past experiences, so no one is right, and no one is wrong. It's just an opinion, a perspective, and that seems to be the biggest problem with everything. Everyone thinks they're right. Everyone reading this thinks they're better than the average driver; it's just the way we're wired.

Time waits for no man, they say. It keeps flowing untethered as our lives do. It keeps moving onwards. But be aware, Bruce—if you make a mistake, if something goes wrong, you cannot turn back time and try it again, so in that sense there really are no genuine second chances. Think about it. No do-overs, as they say.

It just makes more sense to be aware that what we decide, what we say, all the small decisions we make every day, such as turning left, turning right, or the things we say, cannot be changed once they happen. We cannot go back and do things differently. Of course, apologies can be given and accepted, but it's better to think twice before you automatically decide upon something.

Sometimes in life, and remember perspectives, we bullshit a lot of people, lie to a lot of people, and try to get what we don't deserve. But the truth of the matter is that you must be careful not to bullshit yourself.

So, let's talk about happiness. How many of you out there have said, "Oh, when I get that raise, when I buy that sweater, when I get that new car—when, when, when! Whatever it is, we want to lie to ourselves about being happy once it happens. *Oh yes, I'll be so happy because I'll be on top of the world then!* The truth of the matter is that the world is round, so you never truly get on top of anything. You lie to yourself. You delay gratification for happiness and keep working without a real goal in mind. Who are you kidding, Kenneth?

The truth of the matter is that happiness comes from within. I can only talk about myself, but use me as an example. I busted my ass 10 to 12 hours a day, six days a week. I had my head down and kept working and when I finally looked up, it was 45 years later. So, what happened to me? I didn't use anything external to make me happy. Back in my working days, I didn't have time to think about being happy or not. The truth of the matter was that I was scared to death I couldn't pay my bills. My happiness came from within, and I realize now that there is tremendous satisfaction in achieving something through hard work.

I don't care what it is. Whether running a lemonade stand or a multi-million-dollar company, it's all the same. Satisfaction, confidence, completion of set goals, and achieving—that's all it really takes. Don't look to everybody else. Don't look at things, don't look for outside judgments. No, happiness comes from within, and I believe true happiness comes from wanting what you have and having what you want. It's no more than that. It's pretty simple. And believe me, at 78 years old, I'm the happiest I've ever been in my life because with all the ups and downs I've had, with all the tremendous successes I've had, and all the absolute failures I've had, it took 45 years to realize I needed to be true to myself, be honest with myself, know I'm not all that much, and even sometimes say to myself, "Hey, I did pretty good."

That's what it takes: effort, determination, and, as you read earlier, following the universal rule. You must work for what you get. Another perspective to keep in mind is that nobody gets out of this life alive. We're all going to die. Sorry to shock you, fellas and girls, but that's just the way it is. So, make the best out of it, take the chances, jump in, dive in, do what you have to in order to seize the day—*carpe diem.* Life is simple. It's awesome, but we all seem to complicate everything. Keep it simple, stupid. You know what that is? That's called a "kiss method." Keep it simple stupid. Why humans want to complicate things, I still don't know, but it doesn't take much. Sometimes you've just got to stand aside from the crowd, look at all the people running around, trying to make this and that in the rat race of life. Just remember, even if you win the rat race, you're still a rat. Is it really worth it?

I can hear your words out there: "Sure, easy for him to say. He's successful; he has money. He lives a great life. But all you people out there—you don't know me; you don't know what I had to go through. I had less than most, but I didn't bitch too much because I was busy trying to survive. I had days when I didn't know how I was going to pay the mortgage. I had days when I knew I could never make payroll unless a miracle happened. Sometimes it did, and sometimes it didn't. I remember one particular night when my next-door neighbor was making noise outside my daughter's window at 3 a.m. She was at a sleepover that night, and I went into her empty room to try to sleep because I'd been tossing and turning all night long.

Why was I tossing and turning? Because I didn't have the money to make payroll. I was looking at life insurance and thinking of killing myself. I didn't know what to do. I remember having the dry heaves and sweating that night, even though the window was open, because I felt so warm, even though it was snowing outside. Then I looked outside at 5 a.m. and saw my neighbors getting into a limousine to go on their vacation somewhere. They were enjoying life, even as I was thinking about the best way to end mine.

I know that's a little dramatic, but sometimes, just when you think it can't get any worse, it does. What would I do? I really didn't know, and then the sun began creeping up for a new day. I realized it was just the way things went sometimes: Tag I'm it, my turn, you're up next. We all get our turn. I don't even remember how I made it through that payroll time, but I did. Sometimes it gets worse, but if you put it into perspective, if you look back and say, "Hey, let me eat this elephant," it works out. And of course you know, the only way to eat an elephant is bite by bite.

I still feel like throwing up whenever I think back on those sleepless nights. So, just remember this: Whatever it is you have to do, it all comes down to whether you think you can or you can't, and whatever you think, you're probably right. It's up to you. You make the decision, and you control your life. You pull your own strings. It's your life, Larry; you only get one chance to decide how you want to live—either in fight mode or flight mode. That's how we're wired.

Lesson to learn:

I think the best lesson is that we realize we are all unique. We all have something to contribute. We all have our own way of doing things; we all have our own way of thinking. That doesn't mean we're right and it doesn't mean we're wrong. Like a friend of mine said, we're all the same, and just a little different. Our world perspective is based on the way we experience life and how we view those experiences. . No one is right and no one is wrong. You have to find what works for you. In my life, I took the road less traveled. I did all those things that others didn't want to do or couldn't do. I chose other directions. They weren't right; nor was I. I just went with my gut. Remember the Harvard study—86% of your gut instinct is correct. Follow your gut. I'm not the smartest guy in the world for sure, and boy, oh boy, did I make mistakes. But I made it. I got through, and now I have perspectives that are unique to me. Again, I'm not right, nor am I wrong. I'm just me, and you are you so don't diminish yourself. Don't listen to the experts; just because the doctor wears a white coat doesn't mean he knows everything, so get a second opinion. Drill, drill, drill down and find out what your truth is. Then make your decision based on you, your facts, and your life. It's your decision, no matter what you do. You can go right, left, up, or down, but you have to live with your decision as it's *your* life.

Don't expect to go to the expert and say, "It didn't work. I don't understand." They're too busy living their own life. Be like the Army slogan that says, *Be all that you can be.* It's a whole big, wonderful world and it's for the taking. If you want it. Don't second-guess yourself; just keep going, and remember a trip of 1000 miles starts with the first step.

CHAPTER TWENTY-FIVE

Hearts Everywhere, Angel Numbers Abound

Even though I believe in the universe, and even though I believe there is a greater being than all of us, I still like to check—just push the envelope a little bit. When I did my taxes when I was still working, I tended to push the envelope as far as I could, but my accountant would always remind me that, "Hey, even though you're pushing the envelope, don't go too far; it's still stationary!

One day, I was walking down the street in downtown Kona, Hawaii looking out at the sea and watching the waves lap up against the shore and the rocks. I decided to play a game to see if there really was a universe, kind of giving it another test as if it owed me something. I was just enjoying the day, and thought I would check the strength of my beliefs, so as I was walking, I decided to think of some way for the universe to show me it's always there. I had already done the blue elephants and that was proof to me for sure; I'd also done a couple of other things like balloons and such, but since I was having a good time, I decided to share some love. So, I said to myself and to the universe, "OK, if you're really out there, start showing me hearts. Show me hearts on the ground, show me hearts in the sky, show me hearts everywhere. I want to know that you really exist, Mr. or Miss Universe, so there!"

I continued on my walk, and then looked down at some of the rocks being splashed by the waves, and sure as hell, there was a perfect heart in the form of some coloration differential on the stones. I laughed to myself.

That was two years ago I believe, when I started to see hearts everywhere, and they are constantly telling me that there is a universe, that they are watching out for me, and that I have someone on my side who is caring for me. It's amazing! In fact, I see so many hearts, we decided that since my wife is a good photographer, we are going to keep pictures of hearts everywhere and post them in our home. We both know what it means to us. To others who view these pictures, I guess it's all about their perspective.

Many times over the months and years, my wife would turn to me and say, "Look at the clock or watch—it says 1:11 or 4:44 or some other repeated number.

Only recently did I ask Jamie what those numbers meant. She replied, "These are angel numbers. It's how the universe lets you know it's always looking out for you." I smiled and finally understood. It's funny—the universe knows it exists. The universe knows more than we know, whether it be a universe or God or some other divine spirit, but it knows better—take it from me. Remember, I wasn't a believer either, until all this weird stuff started to happen to me. We should be laughing at ourselves rather than at what's out there.

I can tell you my life has been an absolute roller coaster, and I've loved every minute of it. I just didn't know that it was being guided, and I didn't know there was a greater good looking out for me for the majority of my life, but that didn't bother the universe. Now, the universe was there before I existed, while I *am* existing, and it will be there even after I'm gone (or at least what I perceive to be a conscious reality). You see, the universe knows what the universe knows; it's us who are on the short end of the stick, so the only way we can even get close is to just believe. Now, as you can see, I like to push the issue from time to time, but it is absolutely uncanny to me that no matter what crazy thought I come up with, the universe will show it to me. Maybe not this moment, maybe not tomorrow, but it will show it to me. Of that I am certain.

Lesson to learn:

The only question I have is: Why did the universe wait so long to wake me up? Or was I supposed to wake myself up? Or maybe it happens when it happens; I don't know but what I do know is that the majority of my life was spent in the darkness of not even thinking about signs from the universe. I think it's an individual thing—you come to the moment of enlightenment when you're ready for it. I think until you have had enough, until you search for a bigger meaning and before you close down, you have to open up . . . and maybe that's it. I think it's an unending question with no answer. It's different for each one of us. I know one thing that's sure: the last ride is the best ride. As they theatrically say, we are riding off into the sunset, and for me and for Jamie, nothing could be more true. We're laughing all the way on the way to it, loving this life of ours.

CHAPTER TWENTY-SIX

Charity with Dignity

While I waited for an Uber, a man sat on the sidewalk, leaning against the wall with the traditional cup sitting beside him, hoping for a donation or a handout while holding a sign saying: *Disabled Vet, please help me.* Of course, many people walked by, more of them ignoring the man than trying to help. And every so often, someone would throw a dollar or some change into the cup for the Vet (if that's what he really was) and he would humbly and quietly thank them or not say anything at all. I thought to myself, *I wonder who's really getting the benefit out of this relationship? The people who are making the gift of change, or the people who are receiving it?* What I mean by that is that sometimes, I think people feel guilty for what they have in life, almost as if they didn't earn it or didn't work for it. Nevertheless, they just hand out a few bucks or a few coins. Do they do it to say, "I'm sorry I'm living better than you, so here's a few bucks to hopefully help you buy something like food or cigarettes or wine or whatever"? I don't know if they're trying to make a difference for the person who needs some money, or if they're trying to alleviate some guilt. I'm not really sure, but I have a better idea. I call it charity with dignity.

Charity with dignity means, rather than throw a few bucks at a down-and-out person, take the time to take them to McDonald's, sit with them and buy a meal for them, get them a haircut, or even better, do something that's going to make a difference. Do something so a person who is truly down and out, and who just needs a break, doesn't feel like a beggar.

There's something I do quite frequently, and you might be able to try it as well. Next time you go to a grocery store and get in line to pay your bill, look at who's in front of you. Do they look like they could use a few bucks or a handout? If so, and you want to help, then before they have a chance to pay, take your charge card out. You can either play dumb and say, "Is this how you pay your bill, with a credit card?" or just do it before they realize what's going on. They'll probably say, "Wait a minute, you just paid for my groceries!" and you'll say, "I sure did. Just pass it on to somebody else." And that, my friend, is a prime example of charity with dignity. Lending a hand up, not just a handout. Think about it.

A study was done by some prominent university in which they wanted to measure the amount of dopamine the brain releases when someone receives a gift and when someone gives a gift. I'm not going to get too technical with you, but let's just say that on a scale of 10 (one being almost zero and 10 being very effective and making a difference), they found that a person who receives a gift will rank anywhere from a five to a six on the scale. That means they get a rush of dopamine at that level when they receive a gift. They also found that the person who gives a gift ranges anywhere from 8 to 10, reinforcing the old adage that it's always better to give a gift than to receive one. Maybe it's even a little selfish, but you get something for giving a gift. It's a kind of interest on your donation. I tried it. It's crazy!

It makes you feel good to help someone and make a difference in their life. Think about it—you can't take your money to the grave, so hopefully you know what you have to do now. Stop thinking about yourself; don't be selfish. Just try it and feel the feeling; that's all I'm asking of you. Just do it one time and if you don't notice it, if it doesn't mean anything to you, then stay selfish and closed-minded. I know you're thinking I'm full of crap but let me share one experience I had that really made me feel good.

One day I went to McDonald's in the morning because I like a good cup of coffee, and I like their coffee. While there, I often do what I mentioned above. I began to look at the people to the right and left of me to see if anyone appeared needy, so I could, as usual, lean forward and tell the person at the cash register to quietly and secretly pay for the person to my left or right. I don't want any acknowledgment. I don't need any acknowledgment. I just try to do a nice thing every day for somebody—a random act of kindness, as they say. So, there I was in line, and I looked to my left and saw a lady with her six or seven-year-old son. They were obviously there for breakfast. He wanted pancakes, and turned to his mother, saying, "Mom, can we have the sausage with that?" She looked in her wallet and said, "Honey, I don't think so. Not this time; maybe next week. I really don't have the extra money." No more was said, and that's all I needed to hear.

I leaned in toward the woman at the counter who was ringing up the order, and said, "There's a woman to my left, in line with her son. When she comes up, make sure I pay for her complete meal as well as her son's. Don't say a word about it. Just do it. I'll ring up and I'm going to walk out, because I think all they want is the pancakes with the sausage, and she wants a cup of coffee and a breakfast sandwich as well." Then I left. I didn't think about it again until perhaps a month or two later when I was in the same McDonald's.

Once again, I looked left and I looked right, and I saw a woman getting breakfast with some other ladies. "Please just ring her bill into my bill," I told the cashier. "Let me get out of here. I don't want anyone to know what I did." But as I was leaving, I didn't even make it to the door. I heard the woman say, "That's the guy—that's the one!"

I turned around, shocked. I thought, *Oh, am I in trouble? Does she think I was hitting on her? I mean, really . . . come on! I'm just trying to be a nice guy.*

She continued, "Yes, you. Come here please, I need to talk to you."

Reluctantly I went up to her and asked, "What's up?"

She immediately said to me, "Two months ago, you took care of me and my son. You bought us breakfast. I was at the lowest point of my life; I'd lost my job, and my husband walked out on me, and I didn't even have enough money to pay the rent. I was at my wits' end. I thought the world was just a shitty place to be, and then you took care of my son and me, you bought us breakfast, and I thought, *Hey, maybe there is some goodness in this world,* and I felt determined to get back on my feet, and I got a new man in my life. I got a better job. And life is getting better and better, and I always think about you and what you did for me and how I never had the chance to thank you, so may I give you a hug and thank you?"

I said, "I don't know about the hug, but you can thank me, no problem." And with that, we both laughed, hugged, and I said, "You're welcome." I left the store knowing I had helped someone and made a difference to someone. And I thought to myself, *It does feel good to have somebody who really appreciates it.*

Lesson to learn:

I find this much better than throwing a few coins into a pot. I feel that each of us exchanging our human frailties goes a farther distance than just a few cents to alleviate some guilt.

CHAPTER TWENTY-SEVEN

Helping Others in Strange Places, Even CVS

You never really know when a helping opportunity is going to present itself. In fact, it could present itself when least expected, as happened to me. Back to Hawaii, fresh from the mainland, we had made the usual round of doctors we see whenever we go back to the Chicago area. We usually carry prescriptions from there to be filled in Hawaii, so as we were coming home from the airport, I remembered the prescriptions, did a quick U-turn, and headed to CVS to drop them off for later pickup.

There was a significant line at the drugstore when I took my place among the others waiting for help. There was a young lady in front of me in line, and when it was her turn she asked if she could speak to the pharmacist. They told her he was busy right then, and asked what they could help her with. She said she was there for the COVID shot, but she had some questions about it before she took it. The clerk said, "If you don't mind waiting out of line, when we're done with all these customers we will be glad to have the pharmacist speak to you and answer any questions you might have about the risk of taking the shot."

I was next, and I just said, "Here are my prescriptions; call me when they're ready and I'll come back and pick them up." The woman who had been standing in front of me looked extremely bothered, and I asked her if I could speak to her for a moment.

"Of course," she said. I told her my wife was a big proponent of NOT taking the vaccine, and that she knew all the research that SHOULD'VE been done on the vaccine but wasn't, and if she wanted to speak with my wife, then she could come outside with me and speak to her.

She said, "Absolutely! I am so confused about taking the shot that I just can't decide. My family wants me to take the shot. I have heard some horror stories, so I just don't know what to do." And then she said it: "Maybe the universe is putting me in front of you for a reason. I'm a very spiritual person, and I believe there is a reason you were standing next to me." She wanted to talk to my wife ASAP.

Outside we went, and when my wife saw me walking out with this woman, she asked what was going on. I explained to her that the woman was having some hesitancy about taking the COVID vaccine and that I thought she could give her more information than I could. "Would you mind talking to her a little bit.? If I can save someone from that damn vaccine, I'll feel good about it."

I also told the woman I had been injured by the vaccine and gotten atrial fibrillation which resulted in a five-hour surgery to fix the damage. I let the woman and Jamie speak for well over a half hour before I said, "Hey guys, we've got to get home already."

All of a sudden, the woman started to cry and said, "Thank you so much—both of you. I'm really scared of injuring myself, and I believe there is a reason that we spoke today. I've decided, I'm never going to take the vaccine, because you two were sent from God, saying don't do it."

This was at a time when the COVID vaccine was starting to be looked at with a querying eye, and the vaccine wasn't all they had told us it was. In fact, they lied to us pretty badly, as it turned out. It was time for us to go, but the woman took both of our hands and said, "Bless you both; you might have just saved my life, so thank you." She went on her way to work, not taking the injection, and we felt better for having helped her make the right decision. Maybe we saved a life or maybe we saved her from not getting hurt by the vaccine. Whatever we did for her, it felt really good to help her with the truth, telling no lies to her like the ones being told to the American public by Big Pharma and our government.

Just another example of the existence of the universe, which is different for all of us. If you're truly open to the signs around us, and you see the same ones I and many others do, don't ignore them. Be aware and think before you act.

Lesson to learn:

There is no special place. There is no temple of insight and there is no right and wrong, if and when, here or there, in or out. It all exists and none of it exists. I'm trying to tell you that you don't have to be in a special place to have the epiphany of a sign or a message coming to you. Don't ignore it. Don't think you can't have this message coming to you in the middle of the grocery store, or a movie theater, or wherever. Yes, you can, buttercup, so strap up because here's a fact: the universe is out there. It's all around us. It will speak to us when it feels the need to speak to us, and it's up to us to listen. So, listen for those messages. Because they're out there loud and clear; the responsibility is on us to pay attention and to think twice before we make a move.

CHAPTER TWENTY-EIGHT

All in 24 Hours

This is going to be my last chapter about things that have happened to me because I think I've gotten the idea across to you. But just in case, enjoy these things that happened to me all within 24 hours (actually, all within 12 hours). As I've told you before, we went to Brazil to attend a friend's wedding and to just look around and see what we could find. We went to a city named Curitiba, which is probably one of the most beautiful cities I've ever seen. It is clean, pristine, and the home of a beautiful designer dress store that my wife had been hearing about ever since we knew we were going to Brazil.

We were planning on getting married in the next couple of months and thought it would be nice to have a designer wedding gown made just for her. One of the thoughts going through my mind was that I had been married for 42 years and then divorced, and my folks never really liked my ex-wife, and come to think of it, I don't think I ever did either. I thought to myself, *Gosh, I only wish my mom and dad could have seen my new wife in her wedding dress and could be with her just for this wedding.* And I thought, *Wow, my dad came from a little city called Kiev in the Ukraine. It would've been nice to have my mom and dad at this wedding, even in a spiritual way.* So, I kept that thought near to me as just that—a thought.

When we walked into the beautiful store with many, many dresses to pick from, I thought to myself, *Oh boy, we're gonna be here all day long.* Then all of a sudden, Jamie looked around the store and pointed to one dress and only one dress. "That one," she said. "I want to try on that dress; something is calling me, and I want to try that dress on."

The woman said, "No problem. That's the dress you think is for you, so let's see if you're right."

So, into the dressing room Jamie went, with the dress and two ladies to help her put it on.

Out of the dressing room she came, twirling around with excitement and enjoyment, saying "Yes, yes, this is the dress for me. It feels so right, and I love the feel and look of it." I had to admit it was a perfect look, and as mentioned before, my wife was a professional ballerina in her day, and a yoga teacher for 25 years, so to say she is fit and trim is an understatement. She has a great figure and knows how to show it off. And in this wedding dress, she knew how to turn it on for sure. It was a form-fitted dress that only a few could even attempt to put on, and it fit her perfectly. I don't think they did more than a few stitches to take it in here and let it out there.

When I say the dress fit perfectly, it did, because when I asked how long it would take to make the alterations, they laughed and said, "Maybe 10 minutes, and that's stretching it, so you can wait for it if this is the dress you want."

The woman who showed the dresses had to agree that this dress looked great, but she urged my wife to try on a few others that she had in mind. My wife being one who always likes to please, said, "Sure. Let me try a few others, but I really like this one." Those other dresses were on and off in just moments. Everybody, including the lady in charge, said, "You're right—that first dress is you." The woman who owned the store came over and shared some information with us. She said, "We just received this shipment three hours ago, and put this dress out as it's from a brand new designer. No one other than you has even tried this dress on; that's how new it is. This is a brand-new designer from overseas, and we are thrilled to handle her."

"Is this Gucci, Prada, or some other high-fashion designer?" I asked.

"No, she is new to Brazil and not available yet in the United States."

"Oh," I said, just being cordial and making conversation as the look on my wife's face told me to get the credit card ready because this dress was now marked SOLD.

"Yes, she is up-and-coming," said the store owner. Her name is Sophia, and she's from the city of Kiev in Ukraine."

I didn't say anything at the time, but you could have picked me up from the ground when I heard the names. You see, my mother's name was Sophie and my father was from Kiev, Ukraine. My parents were going to be at the wedding after all, so close to my wife's heart and surrounding my beautiful wife. Thank you, universe.

After the credit card was presented, everyone was happy and excited, so we decided it was well past lunch and we were all hungry. Caught up in the excitement, we had forgotten to eat. So, we went to the nearest mall, and not knowing one place from the other, we wandered around and saw a restaurant that looked pretty nice, and entered. Of course, I forgot about the language problem. It's not so easy to say you want this or that when the menu and everything is in a foreign language. Nevertheless, not being shy, I asked for a manager. A gentleman came up and asked if he could help us. His name was Sergio. His English was good. I asked him where he learned English so well, and he said, "Miami Beach." That was where he visited his daughter from time to time, and he practiced his English there.

Sergio said, "I'm here and I'm the owner." And as he was trying to understand that I wanted to order from the menu, he noticed my Star of David necklace and we realized we had more in common than we'd both thought. I found out when he was going to be in Miami next and made arrangements to meet him and his family there, as we were going to be there at the same time. Unfortunately, our schedule changed and we weren't able to meet him. We have been in Curitiba three times since that day, and whenever we are there, we always look up Sergio and the restaurant. He's one of those friends with whom you just pick up where you left off. Great guy. Isn't that weird that sometimes, just in a casual meeting, you find somebody to become friends with, and they have a lot in common with you even though they might be on the other side of the world?

Hopefully this book has been an introduction to the universe for you. I know if I had told you I was going to write a book about a third dimension out there that influences us every day of our lives, you would think I was crazy. But that's OK. It works for me, and I know it will work for you. So, why don't we just summarize it?

Yes, it's time we wrap this book up, because this book isn't the end. It's just the beginning for you. I'm sure there will be more books written, but this is the primer. This is the beginning of what this magical universe is all about.

Often, as I go down my individual path in life, I think to myself, Is it just me who knows about the universe? Is it something we learned? Does it just present itself to us? It's really crazy, the different ways the universe tries to direct us. Don't overthink this; whether you like to believe it or not, the universe exists. End of story. It's kind of like music. Sometimes music is just that, music. Enjoy it, turn it on, turn it off, make it louder, make it softer. And yet other times . . . it has a message that is loud and clear, and I receive it. I get it. I understand. So, thank you, universe.

I have tried to teach you about signs. Some are very subtle, some are right in your face, and sometimes, just knowing there is a universe out there protecting you is a very comforting feeling. Now, you are either believing everything I have told you or you think I'm full of crap, and that's OK. This universe thing works for me. I don't know if we grow into learning about the universe or if it presents itself as something so mystical we are dazed by it. I think it's different for everybody. I think some people never hear about the universe, never tune in, and are too busy with the rat race of life, trying to be the winning rat.

It was helpful for me to write this book because it seems to have put things in order for me. I understand that in life words are said, feelings can be hurt, and perceptions can be skewed. But when it all comes down to it, we come into this world with nothing, and we leave with nothing, and that's OK. It seems to balance everything out.

For some reason, and I don't know why I remember this, but I recall my dad telling me a story when he was working. My father was a public accountant (not a CPA). He specialized in doing accounting for independent hospital groups. My father traveled quite a bit during his working years, and he related a story about when he was in Fargo, North Dakota. Fargo was not known for many things, but one thing that stands out is its winters, and the winter my father spoke of was no different. That winter, he was stuck sharing a room with a priest from the hospital. My dad and the priest were stranded at the hospital because of 20 inches of snow, with nowhere to go. Dad was a philosophical kind of guy, always looking for some esoteric meaning about the reality he was living. He turned to the priest and asked him, "Father, what is life all about?"

The priest hesitated for a moment and then said, "You know, I think if I had to sum it up, life is all about balance. We live, we die, we laugh, we cry. It's all about the breakdowns, family and friends, acquaintances, and strangers. Every day we make decisions; every day we choose paths, and every day we take our path because there's no road so sweet as the one we have taken in the past. Going down that lonely road opens so much to us."

But remember, if you're not open to the universe, then it's just a road.

Two men were in prison. The prison was located in a very dry area—a place with a couple of cacti, a few flowers, and that was it. Each man had his own cell. Their only contact with the outside world was a barred window that allowed each of the men to look out at the environment they were living in.

One man looked out and all he saw was the searing heat of the desert. He saw a few cacti and a couple of rocks and complained every day about his dire situation. Interestingly, though the other man looked out through a similar window in his cell, and he saw the shadows the cacti would make; he saw the sunrise, the sunset, the beauty of a mist, beautiful clouds, rain, storm clouds, beautiful sunlight, and then of course, the evening, just when the Earth is settling down for a rest, and he took in the smell of the setting. He also noticed a few birds flying, a couple of lizards crawling, and some ants trying to get some food to bring down to their den.

Maybe I have stirred something in you, and maybe you're bursting with wanting to say it's their reality. It's their perspective. One sees a dire, miserable existence and the other looks out a similar window and sees a beautiful environment with seasons changing, animals crawling, birds flying, and that life is good.

PERSPECTIVES

This book was your introduction to the universe and what you do with this information is up to you. It feels good knowing that somebody has my back. I can't tell you it's God, and I can't tell you what the feeling is, really. It's just a feeling, and maybe when you get to where I am, you will enjoy it as much as I have.

Remember all I have told you; try to keep it as simple as possible. Do some of the tests we've talked about—ask the universe to prove itself to you. It's fun, and I have yet to be disappointed. Life is wonderful. The right partner in your life is even better.

Remember, you are not alone in this world, even if you are. The universe watches over all of us and when you're looking at humanity, maybe like the song says, maybe God is represented as just a slob like all of us. We are all God's children. We are all here for a reason. We are all part of the microcosm, which makes the universe what it is. I think I'm beating this message into you as best I can. There's no point in repeating it over and over again. There is a universe whether you wish to recognize it or not. There is a greater power than us, whether you wish to recognize that or not. Know that this world is too perfect of a place for there not to be some power greater than all of us.

I hope you enjoyed this book, and that I didn't make it too crazy with my stream of consciousness. I guess I suffer from ADHD, and my brain just goes from place to place with my thoughts, so I apologize if I bothered you or bored you, but I think it has been an interesting read for you. I know it was interesting for me to write. Enjoy, my friends. Thanks for buying the book. I could use the money!

ABOUT THE AUTHOR

SHELDON (SHELLY) GOLDNER grew up on the West Side of Chicago in an area called Austin, where life was simple and a quarter bought a hot-dog, fries, and a drink at Carl's. High school was rough, but college turned things around when he was given a probationary shot at junior college. He rose to the challenge, went on to earn his bachelor's degree, and spent three years in law school before being drafted into the Army for four years.

After losing interest in law, Shelly joined his ex-father-in-law's seafood business "just for a few months," which turned into 13 years of wild ups and downs. Eventually, he started his own business with little more than an idea and no money. That leap began the unpredictable ride that inspired *Isn't That Weird!*—a book filled with wacky, wonderful, and tear-jerking lessons learned along the way.

Shelly shares life as it is: real, raw, and unapologetic. His stories aim to wake readers out of their stupor and help them see the world as it truly is. Still learning every day, he embraces each moment with Jamie, his happily ever after, and invites readers to dive into this thing called life with him.

Aloha